STREET-
SMART
CAREER
GUIDE

Best wishes for Success!

L Pedersen

Also by Laura Pedersen

Play Money (Crown, 1991)

STREET-SMART CAREER GUIDE

A Step-by-Step Program For Your Career Developement

LAURA PEDERSEN

CROWN TRADE PAPERBACKS
NEW YORK

Published by Crown Publishers, Inc., 201 East 50th
Street, New York, New York 10022. Member of the
Crown Publishing Group. Random House, Inc. New
York, Toronto, London, Sydney, Auckland

CROWN is a trademark of Crown Publishers, Inc.

Manufactured in the United States of America

Library of Congress Cataloging-in-Publication Data
Pedersen, Laura.
      Street-smart career guide : a step-by-step program
   for your career development / Laura Pedersen. —
   1st ed.
          p.   cm.
      Includes index.
      ISBN 0-517-88037-7
      1. Career development.   2. Vocational guidance.
   I. Title.
   HF5381.P33   1993
   650.14—dc20   92-42690
                                                      CIP

10   9   8   7   6   5   4   3   2   1

First Edition

For William

Contents

Acknowledgments   ix
Introduction   xi

Part I. Career Planning for Tomorrow's Marketplace
1. **George Jetson Would Be in Shock**   3
   • The Information Age   5
   • High Technology   7
   • The Rise of Mass Media   13
   • The Consumer Revolution   16
   • Environmental Awareness   19
   • Social Consciousness . . . for Profit   26
   • Privatization   29

2. **The Rise of Global Consumerism**   37
   • Communism or Coca-Cola?   37
   • International Markets   39

3. **Being a Career Entrepreneur**   44
   • Combining Your Life with Your Work   44
   • What Is a Career Entrepreneur?   45
   • How to Start Thinking Like a Career
     Entrepreneur   47
   • What Fields and Companies Should You
     Examine?   51

4. **Seeing Problems as Opportunities**   62
   • Social Problems   62
   • Easing Crises   64
   • Filling Lacks   67

Part II. A Step-by-Step Plan for Career Development
5. **What to Do with Your Life If You Decide
   Not to Join the Army**   77
   • Finding Your True Calling   78
   • Some Common Occupational Pitfalls   82
   • Encouraging Change   87
   • Developing a Personal Style   88

6. **Do for Pay What You Would
   Do for Play**   89
   • Doing What Comes Naturally   89
   • Navigating Your Route   92

7. **Homing in on Specific Fields**   98
   • Where the Jobs Are   99
   • Selecting an Occupation   107

8. **Starting on Your Way**   113
   • Getting the Inside Scoop   113
   • Real People   117

9. **Planning for College and Considering
   Graduate School**   120
   • Education: What It Can and Can't Do
     for You   120
   • What to Study   126
   • Should You Take an Advanced Degree?   126

10. **Work for Free**   129
    • The Importance of Experience   129
    • Developing an Internship   130
    • The Do-It-Yourself Program   132
    • Making Free Work Pay Off   135
    • How to Finance Working for Free   135
    • Making the Most of Your "Internship"   136

11. **Finding a Job**   141
    • Getting Your Foot in the Door   141
    • Locating Employers   144
    • Making Contact   148
    • Presentation   151
    • Once You're In   153
    • Play It Safe   155

12. **Street Smarts**   156
    • Parting Perspectives   156
    • Thoughts on "Success"   158
    • A Few Words on "Failure"   160

Resource Guide   163

Index   169

Acknowledgments

I would like to give special thanks to my energetic and attentive editor, James O'Shea Wade; my literary agent, Robert I. Ducas; and Miranda Spencer, whose input on style and substance has made this a better book.

Introduction

When I graduated from high school and left my hometown of Buffalo, New York, to pursue a career on Wall Street, I was a determined, though broke, eighteen-year-old. I had no money and no family connections, so I got the only job I could, as a gofer on the floor of the American Stock Exchange. Two years later, at twenty, I became the youngest person in stock market history to have a seat. At twenty-one I became a partner in a Wall Street firm and earned a finance degree by attending New York University at night. Two years later, having combined the trading skills I'd learned with business know-how, I was able to retire as Wall Street's youngest millionaire.

A week after leaving Wall Street I entered the television industry as an intern at "The Joan Rivers Show." After three months of learning the business, I became Ms. Rivers's personal assistant. While working for Rivers, I wrote and published my first book, *Play Money: My Brief But Brilliant Career on Wall Street*, which offers an insider's view of the way Wall Street *really* works. Today I make my living as a speaker and financial consultant.

In looking back on these career accomplishments, however, I certainly don't consider myself exceptional; and I don't credit luck, transcendental meditation or megavitamins either. It was all common sense, probability, and a *plan*.

Back when I was a teenager trying to find a career that would combine my interest in business with an opportunity to get rich, I read a multitude of self-help, career opportunity, road-to-success, how-to-become-a-millionaire, and personal motivation books. After trying all the theories presented—including sleeping with a piece of paper with my goal written on it under my pillow—I soon realized that none of these guides offered any practical advice, concrete steps, or realistic planning for the world as we know it. There was too much goal-setting, abstract jargon, and wishful thinking—*without* enough simple, straightforward advice for the average person. After a few years of successes and failures, I developed my own comprehensive, concrete, credible strategy—one that works.

Street-Smart Career Guide is a synthesis of motivational speeches I have presented from coast to coast on the topic of choosing and pursuing a successful career in a rapidly changing international marketplace. Here you'll find a creative new approach for turning almost *any* job into wealth and fulfillment—practical ideas and simple procedures to follow. Whatever profession you choose, from day-care-center worker to nuclear physicist, the secret of success is to integrate thinking (and often behaving) like an *entrepreneur* in your daily routine or job.

This book will *not* advise you on such mundane tasks as resumé writing and salary negotiation, or tell you what hairstyle or outfit works best at a job interview. Many other books address just these subjects. Nor will you find pages of strange, arrogant, or philosophical career advice. I'd never tell you to walk into the president's office and proclaim that you're indispensable, hire a limousine to deliver your invention to a company, send the personnel department flowers with a resumé tucked among the baby's breath, or chant "I will succeed" in the shower. I'm not going to tell you to smile and have good posture — or even a good attitude, for that matter. I've met New York City taxi drivers who had better so-called attitudes than many successful CEOs.

The suggestions that follow simply state how to narrow your interests, locate the best career opportunities, and exploit them in a way that will make you financially secure *and* happy.

I believe there's no reason to go through life muttering, "I hate Monday," "Wednesday is hump day," and "Thank God it's Friday." You don't have to be born with a silver spoon, have *Mayflower* family connections, be an Ivy League graduate, or have a straight-A transcript to discover how to approach any job through the back door — and maybe even become a millionaire, too.

PART I

Career Planning for Tomorrow's Marketplace

1

George Jetson Would Be in Shock

In the midst of the economic turmoil of the 1930s, the pioneering economist John Maynard Keynes predicted that when everyone had a four-bedroom house the American Dream would be fulfilled and people would lose their incentive to work. As we now know, just the opposite has happened. As Paul Zane Pilzer wrote in his 1991 book *Unlimited Wealth*, "The more we earn, the more we spend; the more we spend, the more we get; the more we want, the harder we seem to be willing to work to earn more money to get it." In other words: Consumer demand is insatiable. And if you don't believe that, go to a Sharper Image store, where frivolous toys for grown-ups command staggering prices and tremendous interest.

To understand the full scope of job opportunities in the United States, you need only grasp and accept one truth: Consumption—the act of purchasing goods and services—can only exhaust itself in a complete economic depression. Fashion designers discovered this hundreds of years ago when they ran out of ideas and started pulling things out of their parents' closets and giving them a new twist. Just when you think the garment industry has hit a creative brick wall, it starts marketing pre-washed, pre-ripped, and pre-patched jeans that scarcely withstand one spin in the dryer but cost twice as much as a sturdy pair of Levi's. What's more, people buy them!

This kind of creative resurrection happens in every industry. The American Dream is purposely made so elusive that even an aggressive consumer doesn't have the slightest chance of achieving it except for a fleeting moment and then the ground shifts again.

Consumption is a never-ending cycle. For example, my grandfather's entire working life was spent securing food and shelter. He immigrated to America after deciding that life on a pig farm in Denmark was not going to be nearly as exciting as waiting on tables in the Wall Street area of New York City. Along with millions of others who passed through Ellis Island at the turn of the century, he started to work toward acquiring the basics. Sixty years of serving smorgasbord earned him enough money to support a wife and raise a child (my father) in a small apartment in a pleasant neighborhood, and eventually to buy a bronze-colored 1980 Camaro.

The next generation is another story: an American family that has earned more money than my grandfather did. They buy a larger house, possibly a boat, go on cruises, and wear expensive clothes. But what do their kids want to do more than anything else in the world? Go camping.

That's right—the family closes up the expensive house, takes food from the fridge, cabinets, and grocery store and packs it into Igloo coolers, and pays a neighborhood kid to feed the cat and dog. Then they go to the sporting goods store and spend a fortune on lanterns, insect repellent, rain gear, a Coleman stove, sleeping bags, and a compass. Finally they often have to pay the owner of a campsite to sleep out in the cold and rain with the ants, bears, and mosquitoes. In other words, millions of American families are paying top dollar every year to achieve what their grandparents spent a lifetime trying to avoid. Consumption is a never-ending cyle.

Another basic truth shines throughout history: Revolutions are more often caused by people wanting washing machines, refrigerators, and toilet paper than by true dissatisfaction with the current political party, as the demise of the USSR has proven. And likewise, the political and economic revolutions of twentieth-century America are connected with people's needs and demands—and will continue to be, as long as *Homo sapiens* walks the earth.

Beneath this flurry of changes lie some fundamental structural shifts. By first identifying the panorama of changes currently sweeping through our lives, you can also discover where today's opportunities lie.

The connecting thread running through the social, economic, and political events of this century is a series of breathtaking advances in science and technology, creating a totally new foundation for the civilization in which we live in the developed world. It's a shift as significant as that from hunting to agriculture in ancient times, and from agriculture to industry in our grandparents' era. In our own time, it is a transition from mechanical industry into what is called high technology or the Information Age.

So when you're preparing for that job in the future, that's also where you have to look: the future! Observe the changing structures. They're evolving right under your nose.

The Information Age
Employment in the U.S. economy is shifting from production (making items such as steel and refrig-

erators) to service industries (health care, education, repair and maintenance, amusement and recreation, transportation, banking, and insurance). The decrease in manufacturing jobs does not represent a decline in industry—quite the contrary, since output has climbed 26 percent in the past 15 years—but is caused by increased productivity gains from better technologies and more efficient operations. For example, in 1992 American steelmakers used, on average, 5.3 hours of labor to make a ton of steel—less than half of the labor required in 1980, according to the May 16, 1992, edition of *The Economist*. The U.S. Department of Labor's *Occupational Outlook Quarterly* (Washington, D.C.: U.S. Government Printing Office, Spring 1992) reports that manufacturing employment has declined from 21 million in 1979 to 19.1 million by 1990, and is projected to decline another 600,000 by 2005. This is quite understandable if you also take into consideration that competition from low-cost foreign labor is driving down the demand for less-skilled workers at home. As a result, most of the projected loss will be in production jobs while the number of professional, technical, and managerial positions will rise.

As we approach the year 2000, increasing numbers of workers are providing services that were not available ten years ago or even, in some cases, last year. Entire industries are being developed simultaneously to produce and maintain the new technology that enables these services to be performed.

Today, everything that consumers want can be ordered at the touch of a button. Car phones, faxes, and on-line computers produce immediate results. People taped CNN's up-to-the-minute broadcasts of the Gulf War as easily as if they were a football game.

The development and increase in use of information technology are reshaping the work force, a trend likely to continue. According to the Labor Department's *Occupational Outlook Quarterly* for spring of 1992, the economy is projected to provide 24 million more jobs in 2005, up from 123 million in 1990. Many jobs will become obsolete, such as typesetting. Demand for word processors will decrease as less paper is shuffled. Only those with initiative will be able to capitalize on the opportunities which will arise.

What has made the Information Age possible? Computers—or rather, technology—the likes of which would make George Jetson's head spin. Computers make information more accessible and less expensive. In turn, those with computer skills will be able to operate profitable businesses, because customers are willing to pay a premium for goods and services that *exactly* meet their needs. No longer is the main objective of the businessperson to create the highest volume for the lowest price. The accessibility of information has revised the challenge; it now lies in finding the right match between available technologies and the potential markets. In other words, a knowledge of the customer's specific needs, together with the ability to meet them, can bridge that gap. As the use of computers by businesses, government agencies, and schools increases, so does the demand for programming, software designing, technical support, analysis, sales, and marketing.

High Technology

Bullet trains, SSTs, and hand-held electronic encyclopedias are no longer Hollywood special effects. Electrically powered cars traverse Southern California highways. AT&T and Vapor Canada, Incorporated, of Montreal are marketing a highway toll-collection system that would automatically deduct tolls from computerized credit cards so that drivers no longer have to stop at toll booths. NYNEX offers a traffic-jam service in which an operator will inform you of any traffic congestion and offer alternative routes. American Airlines uses applied-intelligence software to schedule the routine maintenance of its airplanes. Pretty soon, when you fly to the West Coast, you will arrive earlier than the time you departed.

These are just a few examples of the more dramatic technological wonders that are quickly becoming part of daily life. Even on a more mundane level, technology provides new possibilities in the ways a product is developed, designed, produced, marketed, delivered, and serviced.

For instance, in 1991 the use of mobile phones increased over 40 percent in the United States and 35 percent in Europe. Electricians, contractors, and realtors no longer worry about receiving calls while out on a job. As companies such as US West, Pacific Telesis, IBM, Infonet, Ram Broadcasting, Bell South, and General Electric build up their electronic communications departments, they create more jobs in sales, technology, customer service, installation, legal departments, and so forth.

Technology has made it possible to distribute a vast array of products to an unlimited number of consumers. The rule in America has been that city-dwellers have always had access to a larger selection of products and could have them in a shorter amount of time, if not immediately. Now, even people in remote Alaskan villages can get pâté from Zabar's and lingerie from Victoria's Secret quickly shipped to them.

Ten years ago, the objective behind a television

or newspaper ad was either to corral you into the store, so that the salespeople could finish the pitch, or to persuade you to decide ahead of time which brand you should purchase. Now businesses are slaves to direct marketing. The point of purchase is shifting from the supermarket checkout line to your favorite armchair in the comfort of your own living room.

How did you buy your gourmet coffee, holiday gifts, rugby shirt, pet's raincoat, or juicing machine? Did you jump in the car and head for a ramble through the packed local mega-mall? Chances are you dialed an 800 number broadcast on TV, mailed in a catalog order form, faxed your order from your office, or even zapped it in via computer modem.

While big retail stores such as Macy's and B. Altman flounder in bankruptcy, catalog sales companies such as Lillian Vernon and Land's End are rapidly expanding and upgrading their order-processing, administration, and customer service to incorporate more computerization. Investors have shown their approval by purchasing stock in these companies.

Another result of technology-driven marketing is that an individual or a very small company can gain access to large markets through direct mailings and computerized inventory systems. All that's necessary is a warehouse. One can operate a sophisticated business with very low overhead out of one's home, and need no longer maintain a fully equipped store with salespeople and adequate parking.

All this, of course, is accomplished by computers. The cost of using computers has fallen dramatically since 1980. Prices continue to fall by around 30 percent a year, according to the January 4, 1992, edition of *The Economist*.

Technology also reduces the amount of labor necessary to provide services. The high wage level in this country has spurred firms to employ any methods that make expensive personnel more productive. As a result, America is the driving force in providing services to an international clientele. In his book *The Competitive Advantage of Nations*, Michael Porter lists the service industries in which the United States has the leading position against significant international competition:

- Fast food
- Graduate education
- Entertainment
- Hospital management
- Car rentals
- Advertising
- Management consulting
- Construction
- Industrial laundry/ apparel supply
- Waste disposal and management
- Credit cards
- Credit reporting
- Commercial banking
- Money management
- Custom software
- Secondary and university education
- Corporate training
- Health-care services
- Hotels
- Accounting
- Public relations
- Engineering/ architectural
- Temporary help
- Consumer finance
- Merchant/investment banking
- Leasing
- Information processing
- Information/data

The production of manufactured goods spurs the demand for these types of services. When goods are sold, needs arise for transportation, packaging, operating instructions, insurance and legal coverage, financing, and possibly ongoing maintenance.

Farther from home, the increasing availability of technology has entirely changed the wealth and status of many nations. Before Henry Ford devised the assembly line, a country's wealth used to be determined directly by its natural resources: land, minerals, energy, water, and so on. International trade worked much the same way lunches are exchanged in elementary school; whoever had the largest amount of the most desirable items was going to win.

No longer. Now a country's productivity is determined by how quickly and efficiently it can harness (or purchase when necessary) natural resources, human resources, and capital goods and then distribute them as products and services through an effective distribution system.

It is essential for a country to maintain a work force of trained, specialized labor in order to compete in the services market. The United States is poised to do this because of its preeminence in unique and specialized educational programs such as hotel schools, entrepreneurial programs, and extensive training in computer programming, along with its vast number of M.B.A. and undergraduate business training programs. Currently, more money is spent on science education in America than in any other country in the world, a margin that is unfortunately declining.

American goods and services are not only in demand in their final form. Our expertise in producing them is also continuously sought after by other nations. According to *Business Week* of December 2, 1991, more than half of the Ph.D.'s in engineering, mathematics, and economics awarded by American universities last year went to non–U.S. citizens. In addition, foreigners earned more than 45 percent of the doctorates in computer sciences, physics, and astronomy.

In his old stand-up comedy routine, Woody Allen claimed that his father was replaced at work by a machine. The machine did everything that his father did, except better. So his mother went out and bought one too. Although this was meant as a joke, being replaced by a machine at work happens frequently. In some cities and towns it's possible to ride the subway, withdraw money at the bank, go shopping, make photocopies, send a package via Federal Express, buy postage stamps, have lunch, and see a movie without ever interacting with another human being!

So how is service and manufacturing growing at such a drastic rate while thousands of jobs once performed by humans have been computerized? Don't let the reduction of unskilled labor fool you into thinking that technology is limiting our opportunities. Quite the contrary. More job opportunities exist today than ever before as a result of increasing technology. One can capitalize on the demand for services that are more in tune with consumers' needs by improving upon existing services and concepts. Any existing business can be made more efficient by devising simple methods to help it make and save more money.

Many new jobs are being created as a result of the "value-added" concept. Simply put, what this means is that with each advance in technology, businesses and individuals switch to new and better products that require maintenance, design, research, information systems, and consulting. Some technological and regulatory changes have even opened up new areas such as pollution control, packaging restrictions, medical care, and on-line banking. The increasing complexity in the way organizations operate will also require more individuals skilled in such areas as planning, management, engineering, information processing, and operations analysis. Changes in the way we purchase, combined with technological innovations in computer shopping, custom product searching, sophisticated ordering systems, delivery, and advertising, will also provide specific career opportunities. Most new jobs will open for programmers, marketers, customer services personnel, information providers, researchers, and data processors. Also in great demand will be professionals with specific knowledge in finance, business communications, law, and computer graphics.

The Rise of Mass Media

Who stokes the world's desire for more, more, more? Mass media!

Any American can be a television star. Think about it: You meet on the relationship show "Studs," then you go on "The Newlywed Game" for additional cash and prizes for saying the phrase "making whoopie." Next it's off to dissolve the hasty union on "Divorce Court," a show that gives testimony and histrionics equal time. Then go on "Inside Edition" for fire bombing your ex-spouse's apartment. Finally, have a facelift in jail and go on "Oprah."

The above scenario, though highly implausible, is entirely possible. The bottom line—literally—is that Americans love the media. Even those intellectuals who don't actually purchase scandal sheets at the supermarket surreptitiously speed-read them in line, leaving the last few copies wrinkled and dog-eared. When fiberoptic lines are connected to homes, even video stores will be obsolete. We will be able to order any movie, television show, encyclopedia page, directory assistance, and eventually dinner all at our fingertips. Hewlett-Packard is producing hardware that will allow consumers to shop and bank using a television remote-control device that should retail for less than seven hundred dollars. If someone combines QVC (Quality, Value, Convenience), a twenty-four-hour, shop-by-phone cable channel that reaches most of our homes, with Federal Express to make the deliveries, supermarkets will become superfluous. As shoppers order their groceries from computer screens in their living rooms, only warehouses or direct distribution systems will be necessary to get the items from the producer to the consumer's home. Aggressive interactive TV companies claim that by 1994 viewers will be using their remote controls to order pizzas (pay-per-chew), bet on horse races, perform electronic banking, participate in game shows, and much more. We'll have reached our civilization's peak! Not!

Consumers eagerly subscribe to cable TV for a larger selection of channels, and to pay-per-view for coverage of concerts and sporting events. In its scant eleven years of existence, MTV has become a powerhouse in the music industry, not only for its advertising clout but for its ability to produce trends and to create demand. Marketers have taken the lead from music videos and now develop almost all commercials and film trailers in the same way, with a combination of music, sound bites, and sexy visual imagery. Nintendo isn't just for kids, either. Almost everyone in a computer-game household can be caught trying to slay the iridescent dragon at some point during the work week.

More monitors will also pop up for bank lines, riders waiting for mass transit, movie theaters, cash register lines at shopping centers—any place where consumers are bored, trapped, and eager to look at whatever's playing on the screen. Advertisers and politicians are willing to pay huge premiums for this lock on consumer attentiveness, just as they once did for newspaper advertising. Television has *become* the international newspaper.

Turner Broadcasting System is working with McDonald's to provide an in-store entertainment network, McTurner, that carries promotions, paid advertising, and a video-game component. Other Turner Private Network projects, the Checkout Channel and the Airport Channel, draw most of their materials from CNN. The Checkout Channel was introduced in February of 1992 in 150 stores throughout the United States. It contains news capsules, advertising, and short features, making the wait on line more tolerable for many impatient shoppers. The Newborn Channel will target new mothers in recovery rooms after giving birth, while the Fitness Channel should be available in health clubs in the near future. Always thinking about future possibilities, Turner jokes about creating a Stoplight Channel or a Restroom Network.

Products such as Multimedia, consisting of interactive audio-video "textbooks," are finding their way into the educational system and replacing antiquated rote learning. With specialized computer programs, students can view documents and illustrations or listen to recordings from contemporary historians. Preparing students for the future with high-tech education will provide the work force with a continuous supply of creative thinkers.

The rest of the world is also clamoring for American media. Entertainment is America's second-biggest net export (behind aerospace) and brings in trading revenues of more than $5 billion a year. The demand for American pop music, movies, books, toys, and theme parks appears to be insatiable. Look at the most sought-after items: new popular rock videos and new-release movies. *Premiere* magazine (January 1992) reports that American films account for more than half of box office revenue throughout the world.

To see blockbusters such as *Terminator 2* and *Home Alone,* the Japanese have to buy tickets days in advance. Fans of rap star Hammer bought all 56,000 seats for his concert at the Tokyo Dome.

The world's insatiable desire for entertainment is creating an avalanche of opportunites. Just as being an assembly-line worker or a bank teller used to be thought of as a typical job, it is becoming more commonplace for the average individual (even in a small town or city far from Hollywood) to make a living from the burgeoning entertainment industry. These jobs take many forms: operating a video store; organizing trips to theme parks as a travel agent; taking tickets at the multi-cineplex; promoting upcoming musical and theatrical events or reviewing them for the media; working at the local stadium where rock groups, entertainers, and sports teams play or perform.

The economy and high-tech media systems don't exist in a vacuum, however. Powerful social forces are shaping the direction they will take.

The Consumer Revolution

In the 1950s, when TV's June Cleaver came home with the groceries, she just happily loaded up on her favorite brand names, without worrying about which companies were destroying rain forests or polluting the Mississippi. Wally and the Beaver didn't have to recycle their trash. Ward didn't know that fried foods were leading him to bypass surgery.

Twenty years later, consumers hadn't changed all that much. Carol Brady didn't make all the kids use sunscreen. Her housekeeper, Alice, wasn't avoiding detergents with lots of chemicals in favor of natural cleansers. Even in the episode where Greg got caught smoking, the surgeon general's mild warning notice was still in microscopic print.

Things are now changing fast. In the nineties, health and environmental regulations abound. Government legislation requiring stricter dissemination of information about products has combined with the campaigns of independent groups to educate consumers in politics, environmental concerns, and health. Not that Ho-ho's and other such individually plastic-wrapped products rife with artificial preservatives are as yet passé; it's just that people have learned to be more discriminating about what they eat, use, and wear. Your neighbor who clamored for the elimination of red M&Ms and maraschino cherries (both containing the dreaded dye Red #2) and MSG would now be considered a caring mother rather than a hippie fanatic.

Today's consumers value healthy lifestyles and products. They are also willing to work and pay for them. We're the healthiest generation in history due to changes in our diet, behavior, and frequency of exercise. People are conscious of trying to eat nutritious foods. In grocery stores, product labels are crammed with the words "high-fiber," "low-fat," and "no cholesterol." Smoking and drinking have become both health and social issues, and many people are voluntarily abstaining from tobacco and alcohol. Nicotine addicts are flocking to doctors in record numbers to get a prescription for transdermal patches. People are switching from cocktails to wine coolers, nonalcoholic beer, and club soda. Exercise has become popular as a means to ward off heart disease and lengthen one's life.

Given the option, consumers will buy a safer product. Companies are responding quickly and are being held accountable when they don't observe safety measures and follow guidelines carefully. Instead of advertising a car as flashy, speedy, or fuel-efficient, companies are touting safety and durability.

As concern for safety has grown internationally, companies such as the Swedish Volvo have quickly capitalized on this marketing opportunity and have seen their market shares increase dramatically. Saab, in its enthusiasm to follow suit, has gone so far as to claim that their safety features will protect you in case you happen to collide with an elk!

People's schedules are usually jam-packed; hence, consumers are pressed for time. They need more services to do things *for* them, or that allow them to do their errands at a more convenient time. This will lead to the rise of more twenty-four-hour businesses and more-flexible working hours as people take graveyard shifts, split schedules, and work at home. This means people will need services such as shopping, haircuts, and medical and legal appointments around the clock. They will use more day-care plans and gladly pay for cafeteria programs. The baby boomers' children are now teenagers and need activity centers, runaway shelters, and drug counseling centers. Discovery Zone, a Kansas City, Missouri–based company that franchises indoor playgrounds, is exploiting the "latchkey kids" niche. By the end of 1991, Discovery Zone had almost two hundred locations where children under twelve could slide into wading pools filled with colorful balls and crawl through plastic piping—for a fee, of course.

Consumers have wised up since the eighties, when flashy ad campaigns and costly, well-placed television spots dominated. They have been forced into educating themselves about the difference between glitz and value, either through their own budgeting or, more often, because of cost-cutting on the part of the industry. Now they want *bargains*. The retailers to which status-conscious shoppers once automatically flocked—chain department stores, full-

price designer boutiques, and upscale restaurants—
are folding as discount warehouses and outlet malls
thrive on the outskirts of major cities. Even prestige
brands such as Estée Lauder, Elizabeth Arden, Cha-
nel, and Christian Dior have begun channeling business through discount retailers.

But nobody's slumming. Consumers now demand
quality. In exchange for increasingly serving themselves (banking with a faceless ATM bank card,
pumping their own gas, and pressing digits on touch-
tone telephone systems that serve as operators, and
self-checkout grocery shopping, for example) consumers are demanding better goods, service, guar-
antees, and more competitive pricing than ever
before. The companies that thrive cater to this new,
sophisticated, high-tech purchaser.

Consumers are choosing generic products over
brand names if they find enough similarities in quality
and a big difference in cost. Store brands can be
found for an increasing number of items on grocery
shelves. However, if the company is acting in a politically or environmentally appealing fashion, the
consumer is willing to dig in and pay more.

Environmental Awareness

Concern for the environment is transforming the
way we live, the way we spend, and the way we do
business. Feeling threatened by the fact that most
resources do not replenish themselves as fast as they
are used, the public is changing its attitude toward
nature from exploitation to conservation, in hopes of
forestalling the type of devastation uncontrolled industry has wrought in Eastern Europe, where some
rivers have been polluted to the point of unusability,
even for industrial purposes.

The economic benefits of having a factory in one's

community don't atone for the higher rates of cancer and birth defects suffered by residents of the Gulf Coast region, northern New Jersey, and upstate New York, where toxic chemicals were purposely dumped or accidentally leaked into the air, soil, and water. Such incidents have led to stricter emissions regulations, cleanups, lawsuits, and fines for offending businesses—not to mention loss of faith by consumers. In addition, problems such as the "greenhouse effect"—caused, in part, by too many chemicals in the air and too few trees to cleanse it—could, if left unchecked, be devastating to everyone, no matter where one lives.

We're moving toward a cleaner, "greener" economy; therefore, companies now at the forefront of ecologically sensitive manufacturing are likely to be the ones who'll succeed into the twenty-first century. Companies and products perceived to be environmentally responsible are the ones now gaining the public's loyalty. People are not just worried about the environment; they're willing to pay more to keep it clean.

The passage of laws such as the 1990 Clean Air Act—and state regulations that are sometimes even stricter—confront business with many new challenges. How will they implement cleaner manufacturing? How will they pay for those changes? Once again, this situation presents a tremendous opportunity: though some jobs may be lost in the transition, hundreds of new industries and thousands of jobs will be created in every field as we strive to clean up and prevent pollution and more effectively manage our national resources.

• Environmental strategist W. David Stephenson, writing in the *Christian Science Monitor* of April 17,

1990, observed, "In reality, companies making environmental leadership a key element in strategic planning improve their bottom lines, become more competitive, reduce future liability risks and can avoid boycotts.... [T]he key ... is a new understanding of efficiency, rethinking corporate practices to reduce raw materials and energy consumption and waste production...." Indeed, major companies have begun to follow such principles. The 3M Corporation has received citations from environmental groups for its modern methods, such as recycling adhesives that used to leave the plants as waste. This company aims to reduce its hazardous emissions 90 percent by the year 2000. Utilities are now emphasizing energy efficiency and encouraging customers to use high-tech, compact fluorescent light bulbs. The Polaroid Corporation evaluates its managers partly by how well they comply with environmental rules.

• The new field of environmental consulting is also growing. According to the December 3, 1990, *Washington Post*, "As more companies find they have to clean up their acts to comply with tougher environmental standards, the business of cleaning up the environment is looking like one of the few growth sectors of the economy." Consultants contract with the government and private industry on finding ways to clean up pollution or dispose of hazardous waste. Increasingly, such remedial work is being eclipsed by something more sensible: pollution prevention. Here, management consultants help industries keep ahead of the regulations.

• Stricter pollution laws will boost certain businesses: manufacturers of catalytic converters, engineering firms, ethanol producers, makers of monitoring equipment, research and development firms, makers of computers and software for information collection and reporting, and so on.

• The *Wall Street Journal* of April 20, 1990, reported that venture capitalists have been moving their investments from electronics to environmentally related start-ups. Between 1988 and 1990, venture-capital firms invested more than $100 million in such companies as Galson Remediation Corp., a Syracuse, New York, company that sells technologies to clean up dioxin and PCBs; and In-Process Technologies, Inc., a California firm that provides industrial waste-processing systems. According to one venture capitalist cited, environmentally related start-up products and services have larger growth prospects than most electronic-technology deals.

• The First Environmental Bank and Trust, in Portsmouth, New Hampshire, was opened in 1991 by a group of businesspeople with backgrounds in banking and environmental services to fill a niche for lending to companies in the environmental industry.

• Biotechnology—the use of living organisms as commercial products—will, in all likelihood, soon replace toxic chemicals for a variety of purposes. For example, biotechnological products may be used to fertilize crops and help conserve water. Bioremediation was used to help clean up an oil slick in Texas several years ago by dispersing microbes to eat the oil. The *Los Angeles Times* of April 22, 1990, reported that the numbers of biogenetic products applying for Department of Agriculture approval are on the rise.

Additionally, the export market for environmental technology such as smokestack "scrubbers" is huge. Eastern Europe needs massive pollution cleanup, and the developing nations will need to build "clean" industry. As *Newsweek* reported on June 11, 1990, global pollution problems offer a chance to export U.S. technologies—which cost less than European models, and thus are more likely to be purchased by cash-strapped nations—not to mention fostering good relations.

For example, International Waste Management Systems has negotiated to build pollution-monitoring systems in Czechoslovakia. Clean-Flo Laboratories, a small Minnesota firm that pumps oxygen into waterways to revive aquatic life, has worked with the Polish government on plans to implement its processes there. General Electric is marketing cleaner power plants to countries once dependent on highly polluting brown coal. Martech USA, an Alaskan company, has arranged to clean up contaminated military sites in Czechoslovakia and Hungary with its special soil-washing machines.

Not all environmentally sensitive business opportunities exist in technical areas. "Green" consumer products are already thriving. The March 29, 1992, *New York Times Magazine* reported that "green marketing is booming—for adults and children alike. Some six hundred new green products were unveiled in 1990, which means such introductions are increasing at a rate twenty times faster than the overall rate of new packaged goods." As an example, the story cites Animal Grahams, crackers made from organically grown flour and packaged in biodegradable cardboard boxes that depict eleven endangered species. The same article reported that teenagers—who not only spend $60 billion a year of their own money, but are tomorrow's adult consumers—are the most avid patrons of environmentally sound products. They not only want what's offered, they're pressing for more. Teenagers are even staging sit-ins and petition drives to persuade their schools to switch from Styrofoam to reusable plastic trays. It was a teenager who ultimately got Star-Kist to switch to dolphin-safe tuna!

Meanwhile, the Real Goods Company, a Northern California–based direct-mail business started by an ex-hippie, is earning big profits from environmentally sound goods and energy-saving devices. Why? People crave products that they don't feel guilty about, but that will do an excellent job.

The Nature Company, possibly the first eco-chain, is poised to go international, opening stores in Europe and Japan. A company riding the save-the-Earth trend (although not financially supporting any type of environmentalist activities), the Nature Company enjoys tremendous popularity. Revenues are skyrocketing from sales of organically made body oils, glow-in-the-dark stars, fossils, and other reminders of the outdoors.

Of course, some companies and products (like Hefty's infamous "biodegradable" trash bag that wasn't) attempt to cut corners by maintaining only the *appearance* of environmental soundness. However, studies have shown that consumers prefer companies and products that really are "green." Buyers can quickly see through the PR. They'll scrutinize labels, and opt for something made of 100 percent recycled materials, or choose nontoxic, citrus-based cleaners and solvents over standard, chemical-laden brands.

Consumers are still sorting through the criteria for "greenness," though, and some distributors, such as Wal-Mart in the U.S. and Loblaw's in Canada, have been able to capitalize on the desire to discriminate between conventional and natural products. Loblaw's has created a store generic brand known as the Green Line. Other stores and organizations in the United States are developing variations on this idea, including special seals of approval. During the summer of 1992 the Food and Drug Administration removed some of the mystery from the green game by establishing guidelines for manufacturers making claims about the environmental merits of their products. Several western supermarket chains have teamed up to create a Green Cross labeling program. Green Cross products must fulfill recycling requirements, for example; standards were developed by a private consultant. One nonprofit organization, Green Seal, chaired by Earth Day 1990 organizer Denis Hayes, was formed in 1990 to test and rate products such as light bulbs, laundry cleaners, and house paint according to their environmental impact. Producers are willing to pay for testing and certification because such labels (specifying, for example, that the product contains a certain percentage of recycled materials or is free from certain chemicals) will make shoppers more willing to buy. This, too, may be a growth field, as companies pay testers to evaluate their products.

Overall, what's good for the environment is good for the work force. The enviromental job payoff will come from many different directions. The global market for environmentally friendly products is worth an estimated $200 billion a year, and that's just the beginning. There is a call for designers and engineers to increase fuel economy and reduce emissions in every type of transportation. We need more electric powered vehicles such as France's TGV bullet train, capable of speeds up to 186 miles per hour. This, in turn, will lead to production of more efficient solar electric cells. Efforts must be made to generate clean-burning hydrogen, which will not contribute to global warming. Every inventor, developer, and producer will strive to win the race by recruiting the best marketing and sales staff available to compete for their share of the profits.

Environmentalism is here to stay. It's also big business that, along with the thousands of specially created positions, will require more managers, environmental lawyers, scientists, regulators, creative problem-solvers, and operators of computerized testing equipment.

Social Consciousness ... for Profit

Companies are starting to act on the knowledge that public-spiritedness is part of doing business. International Paper, for example, allows a certain portion of its forests to be used for recreation. Tropicana Products, Incorporated, a leading U.S. producer of orange juice, received the acclaim of former President Bush for its Drug-Free Workplace program, which encourages safety and productivity by randomly testing workers for drug use. Job applicants take a mandatory drug test. A worker can, however, at any time, admit to having a drug problem. In this event the company sponsors and financially supports that individual through the rehabilitation process. Otherwise, if an employee fails a random drug test, he or she is immediately dismissed.

More American consumers are ardently supporting merchandisers of good causes. People began switching phone service to MCI because the company was offering to donate 5 percent of monthly telephone bills to one of four major conservation groups. Visa and MasterCard have introduced cards that allocate a small percentage of the bill to nonprofit organizations. Make-up Art Cosmetics is one company with more than a social conscience. Not only does it raise funds for AIDS research and denounce testing of cosmetics on animals—it's installed a recycling program that rewards customers with a free lipstick for every six containers they return.

On the other hand, consumers are firmly rejecting the products of companies involved in any sort of scandal or unsavory business practice. When wrong-doing is uncovered, the media has consistently made three-ring-circus examples of perpetrators such as Salomon Brothers, instead of allowing them to be fined quietly or slapped on the wrist. Such high-profile issues are forcing leaders, politicians, CEOs, and consumers to act accordingly. Offending firms are now starting to amend their practices. They know that in today's business climate, negative PR can neutralize or damage the positive effects of advertising and marketing, and thus be even more costly than fines and legal fees. Look how rapidly Star-Kist and Chicken of the Sea responded to consumer concern and environmentalists' boycotts of tuna caught by methods that killed dolphins. Now they only purchase tuna caught with dolphin-safe nets. As environmental decency becomes profitable and valued by American society, I am hoping—and betting—that the trend to support good-citizen companies will be followed by an overall rise in business ethics.

And profitable it is:

• The Body Shop, the expanding personal-care products chain, founded by Anita Roddick, is an example of an entrepreneurial venture that embraces political, social, and environmental causes. Roddick's merchandising principles include everything from catalogs emblazoned with "Save the Earth" and "Give Trade, Not Aid" to handing customers a recyclable paper bag with an application to join Amnesty International, an organization that helps to free political prisoners and stands up for humanitarianism. Roddick has transformed The Body Shop from a single boutique in Brighton, England, selling thirteen home-made beauty concoctions, into a billion-dollar business with 634 stores (fifty-six in the United States) and a product line containing more than 350 items.

• Stores are using political activism as a marketing strategy. Esprit de Corp, the San Francisco clothing maker and retailer, registered voters in seventeen of its stores across the United States. The menswear manufacturer Members Only devoted its $3.5 million fall 1992 advertising budget to advertisements encouraging voter registration.

• Working Assets Long Distance, a San Francisco-based long-distance telephone service, gives subscribers free calls to lobby for selected issues. They also sponsored a mailing to legislators in order to support the Freedom of Choice act.

• The South Shore Bank in Chicago is trying to revive an economically depressed urban area and turn a profit at the same time. The company started a local bank and created a for-profit real-estate development company and a nonprofit community development company that works with the bank. The real-estate company offers the possibility of profits, with some risks, and the community development company obtains government and private grants. The need to provide economic opportunity in decaying urban areas has been illustrated vividly in the aftermath of the riots in Los Angeles.

• In finance, mutual funds such as Parnassus, which invest only in socially conscious companies, are on the rise and have often achieved outstanding performance. Such plans include normal types of businesses in their portfolios—banks, computer manufacturers, and steel companies—but omit any that, for example, sell alcohol or tobacco products, or build nuclear weapons. The funds further evaluate a company's labor relations, environmental record, and the like, to make their selections. The formula seems to work: Parnassus, at least, has earned an average 51.9-percent annual rate of return between 1990 and 1991. No one can promise that these types of financial products will continue to do well, but they appear to have great potential. For example, companies with good labor relations are less likely to experience a strike by workers—a situation that causes stock prices to fall. So these types of funds have special consumer appeal: you can make money and sleep well.

The result of the trend in social consciousness will be the reopening of all markets to newer, less established players. If you can come up with a more just, humane way to do business—not even, necessarily, a more efficient or less expensive way—you'll find consumer support. This trend will prove a tremendous windfall for the small-business operator or individual innovator who does not have the benefit of cost-saving mass production and distribution. It is now possible to appeal to consumers' *minds*.

Privatization

Think about some of the scary concepts that have drifted into our vocabulary—global warming, nitrates, carcinogens, the ozone hole, and ultraviolet rays—words that conjure up frightening scenarios of the future, in the manner of old "Twilight Zone" episodes. Now run through *this* list of monsters menacing us *in the present:* registering a car at the Department of Motor Vehicles, dealing with the Internal Revenue Service, opening a bank account, applying for a student loan.

Anyone older than sixteen has experienced the horrifyingly confusing forms that have to be filled out in triplicate just to prove to the government that you exist; the never-ending frustration of being transferred on the phone six times (with twenty-minute hold periods in between), only to end up speaking with the person who originally took the call; and the aggravating endurance test of shuttling from Line One to Window Six, then to Line Three, and so on.

The government of the former USSR was legendary for such red tape and overwhelming bureaucracy. But here in the U.S.A., I believe our own government has done its share of gumming up the marketplace.

Why is it that when unemployment is high, the voters cry out for *government* to create more jobs? During the Great Depression, Uncle Sam offered up employment fare to the masses, such as programs to build roads, bridges, and power plants. There was even a Federal Writers' Project for those less mechanically minded. More recently, the Comprehensive Employment and Training Act, a Nixon administration idea, financed both public works and 750,000 jobs with cities and nonprofit organizations during the 1970s, most of them during Carter's presidency. As stopgap measures they were helpful, but certainly they weren't the kind of solutions that could raise employment levels permanently.

The U.S. Postal Service is a phenomenon unto itself. The average first-class letter now takes 22 percent longer to reach its destination than it did in 1969. Yet, the post office projected deficit for 1992 alone is $2 billion. And unlike workers in corporate America, letter carriers aren't getting any perks, such as limousines for their routes, lunch at fancy restaurants, or an American Express Card.

Now ... what if someone gave the Postal Service to Domino's Pizza? They'd make sure that if a letter didn't get to its destination within a half hour, you'd get the stamp for free—or a dollar off your next order! Give the task of building the next generation of nuclear weapons to the post office. We won't have to worry about Armageddon again for about twenty or thirty years.

Privatization simply means taking a government-run service or industry and turning it over to the private sector through sale, auction, or licensing agreement. Government-regulated agencies are renowned for unnecessary costs, protectionism, and a lack of innovation. Because they are faced with competition, private enterprises have a big financial incentive to improve service, cost, and quality, and to pursue international business.

When a business is privately operated, and its ways of doing things succeed, everyone, from the bankers and entrepreneurs to the non-unionized work force, benefits. The government can actually create more advantages for employment and economic productivity by divesting itself of many of its responsibilities.

In the United States there is still room for much more privatization, even though most industries are already run by the private sector. In the past ten years the government has provided jobs and opportunities for innovators, entrepreneurs, and diligent workers through deintegration. Areas that are slowly being forsaken by the government include education, waste disposal, and the management of correctional facilities. Hospitals, mass transportation, libraries, and other such facilities will continue to pass into the hands of the private sector. (Already half of all the bus routes in San Diego County, California, are operated by private contractors). Attempts to fight this trend only result in losing battles such as the Postal Service has experienced as Federal Express, UPS, DHL, and other express delivery services have demonstrated their higher rate of efficiency by going into direct competition with the government.

Health care is yet another area in which private companies are finding ways to outperform government structures through cost-efficiency and sensible management.

On January 20, 1992, *Forbes* magazine cited Integrated Health Services and Vencor, Incorporated, as two such examples. Integrated has nineteen medical specialty units that offer intensive nursing care to patients who would otherwise be in a hospital, such as persons in coma. Integrated is able to charge 30 to 60 percent *less* than a hospital because it does not provide full-time doctoring or emergency-room services. (Of course, it does not accept Medicaid or uninsured patients.) Private insurers are approving the facility on a case-by-case basis, but finding the savings encouraging enough to increase their support.

Vencor runs seventeen specialty hospitals for ventilator-dependent patients and gets about 75 percent of its patients from hospital intensive-care units. The result is the same: big savings for whoever is picking up the tab and more beds available for patients who need the sophisticated or emergency care that only a hospital can provide.

In other industries the government is quickly encouraging private-sector participation. The law allows private developers to recoup their investment by collecting tolls on roads, bridges, and tunnels that receive federal highway funds (except the Federal Interstate Highway System). This arrangement should result in a "win-win" situation as the nation's infrastructure is rebuilt or upgraded without further draining of public funds, while giving private road-building and engineering firms the opportunity to make a reasonable profit.

In midtown Manhattan a cleanup operation is managed by local businesses. The project is called BIDS (Business Improvement Districts), and takes mandatory taxes on businesses within each boundary and uses the proceeds for security, garbage collection, and street improvements. It employs 185 people and manages its own staff and budgets with money that would have otherwise been allocated by the government.

The rush to privatization is also resulting in once-in-a-lifetime opportunities for those recognizing chances to get in on the ground floor of huge service industries. For instance, Wackenhut Corporation, a Florida security company, manages nine prisons and expects its government service jobs to grow at an annual rate of more than 10 percent over the next decade.

It is a possibility that education will soon take the form of a voucher system whereby schools (and the teachers in them) will get money only if they attract pupils. Nonperformers will eventually be closed down, and students will take the voucher (issued free by the state) to the school of their choice. The Edison Project, started by entrepreneur Christopher Whittle and joined by Benno Schmidt, formerly president of Yale, hopes to build one thousand private schools by 2010. The money saved by reducing the number of teachers, through implementing high-tech learning aids, is supposed to hold costs to the level now spent in public schools and still allow for a profit. The Edison schools are supposed to be open to all, with scholarships available to 20 percent of their students.

Global privatization is taking place at an incredible rate in countries where centralized government long stagnated growth. Just a few years ago, banking in the Soviet Union was controlled by two state agencies. Now dozens of commercial banks have been organized to absorb the surge of independent business ventures. According to the January 4, 1992, edition of *The Economist,* in 1987 there were only six banks (in addition to the central bank), as compared to 1,500 now.

The Treuhandanstalt, the state agency privatizing the former East German economy, sold 3,800 companies to private investors in the first ten months of 1990.

Russian President Boris Yeltsin decreed on July 1, 1992, that all state enterprises must eventually be turned into joint-stock companies (excluding producers of nuclear weapons and space systems). The objective is to transfer ownership of approximately 130,000 large enterprises and thousands of small businesses into private hands.

Railways around the world have recently been opening up to private investors. The Netherlands is planning to raise private funds for a new freight line from Rotterdam to Germany. Argentina is in the process of privatizing all of its railways, including the Buenos Aires metro. Japan has 120 private rail companies, which make up a third of the country's network.

In the People's Republic of China, the inefficiency of state-run enterprises is forcing the Communist Party Central Committee to condone private businesses—whether they want to or not. That's why you'll find McDonald's stores in China's Guangdong Province—identical to American franchises from the fries right down to the polyester uniforms. The government is dependent upon the tax revenues from non-state-run companies to ensure continuation of the Party. This capitalistic source of revenue compensates for the huge losses resulting from China's poorly run industries, and consumer boycotts of them. When given a choice, Chinese consumers are rushing to buy the superior goods offered by the private companies. Capitalistic activities such as stock markets and the buying and selling of real estate are part of the daily routine and no longer considered experimental in China's coastal provinces.

Privatization will continue. Profit is a tremendous incentive to operate efficiently. Global privatization raises commerce levels in these countries, thus providing more fertile markets for American exports. In 1991 the United States, the world's largest exporter, sold a record $422 billion worth of goods and $145 billion in services abroad. Each billion dollars of exported merchandise generates approximately twenty thousand jobs.

As can be seen from privatization, changes that are sweeping the United States also have global ramifications. We live in a global economy in every aspect from politics to the environment, from who's in charge of the country to what types of fertilizer we use on our grass. Our new interdependence indicates that international business often lends itself more easily to cooperation than do politics, philosophy, and religion. In other words, money is getting more votes than ideology.

In fact, the days of economic issues being left under the umbrella of a greater political agenda are over. Economic relations between the United States and other countries are being treated more and more as separate issues. Global takeovers, foreign trade, international participation in local stock exchanges—all of these represent the economic override of treaties, quotas, leaders, elections, and policy-making.

2

The Rise of Global Consumerism

Communism or Coca-Cola?
The world is getting smaller, yet the markets and
opportunities for enterprising individuals are growing
and expanding.

At the beginning of this century, the five or six
democracies in the world were all grouped around
the Atlantic Ocean. Now capitalism is quickly surg-
ing into areas where, only a few years ago, dictators
and bureaucrats made all decisions regarding consumption and production.

The end of the Cold War offers a perfect example
of the increased consumer desire to acquire every
product or service known.

Economists predict that the Soviet economy will
be in a shambles for possibly the next decade. Infla-
tion is high, the ruble is devalued, there's political
turmoil, and food shortages persist. The long-term
outlook, however, is excellent. It will be a long process, but many changes are in place already.

In May of 1991, the opening bell rang at the
brand-new St. Petersburg stock exchange. Primitive
commodity exchanges have been appearing since the
summer of 1990. Many former Soviet companies are
reviving or restructuring themselves through the sale
of stock. When they consider the current rate of in-

flation, the nation's citizens are eager to buy the shares, since the stock will most likely prove to be a better investment for them than putting money in savings accounts. All these moves towards a market system should benefit the economy and spur demand for goods created abroad, as well as provide a tremendous arena for outside investment.

In the new Commonwealth of Independent States, big cities are experiencing a real-estate boom. The prices of one- and two-bedroom apartments are doubling within six-month periods, and office space leases for about seventy-five dollars per square foot — more than three times New York City's rate! With this type of demand, construction, along with other business opportunities, should expand most dramatically. Every ruble earned can then be spent on other goods and services and thus continue going into the cash registers of the local communities.

American companies are creating hundreds of joint ventures a month with the CIS. *The New York Times* appeared in a Russian-language edition in Moscow on April 28, 1992. New air routes are connecting California and Alaska with far-eastern Russia. Polaroid's factory in Obninsk, set up in July 1989, produces circuit boards for the company's instant cameras. Polaroid also has a small camera-assembly plant and a shop in Moscow. Pepsico employs 270 people at its two Moscow Pizza Huts, which it opened in September 1990. Pepsico has also franchised thirty-five Pepsi-Cola bottling plants throughout Russia, under a 1974 agreement that gave it the right to export Stolichnaya vodka. The company expanded its presence in the Ukraine in October of 1992 by signing an agreement to build one hundred Pizza Huts and five new Pepsi bottling plants. The investment capital will be raised through the sale of $1 billion worth of double-hull tankers built with

Ukrainian joint-venture partners. The Ukraine's 52 million people drink the equivalent of 240 million eight-ounce servings of Pepsi a year, a market that the company thinks can be greatly expanded.

In this climate of internationalism, the former superpowers and their rivals are finally exhibiting cooperation rather than simply threatening each other. You don't have to read *The Financial Times* to know that during the earlier part of this century, Japan didn't own nearly as much real estate or as many buildings and businesses in the United States as it has now acquired. Kuwait would likely be a U.S. ally even if we hadn't helped drive out occupying Iraqi forces, since Kuwait has tremendous financial holdings here.

Peace and disarmament here and abroad will greatly alter the U.S. economy. Having grown up near Niagara Falls, an enormous hydroelectric power center—and therefore one of the top targets for a nuclear attack during the Cold War—*I* am certainly looking forward to this. (I'm also still curious to know how seventy third-graders crouched under the coat rack in an elementary school hallway with their heads between their knees were supposed to be protecting themselves from a missile.)

Driving our economy with the so-called military-industrial complex no longer seems justifiable and is being reconsidered. Someday there may even be a small "peace dividend" to channel money from the defense budget into social programs. Conversion of high technology to civilian purposes and utilizing the great minds once dedicated to building bombs to solving other problems is an exciting possibility.

International Markets

As peace "breaks out," our access to the world economy will increase. Not only is the United States cutting back military expenditures, owing to changes in the former Soviet Union, but it is now pulling nuclear weapons out of South Korea and withdrawing troops and closing bases in the Philippines. At the same time, Washington is demanding greater access to trading in Asian markets, especially in Korea, Indochina, Singapore, and the People's Republic of China. Economic globalization is resulting in more trade, more opportunity, and greater prosperity.

As economic considerations transcend political ideologies, trade barriers are also beginning to disappear between North American, European, South American, and Pacific Rim countries.

Chile, for example, began a market economy in the 1980s with extraordinary success. Now Brazil and Argentina are trying to resolve political problems so they can also open their doors to foreign competition. Mexico is busy hammering out trade agreements with the United States and Canada. Mexico's productivity is skyrocketing, while tariffs have shrunk from 100 percent a decade ago to 20 percent today. African nations are considering drastic economic reforms that would allow less government regulation of trade and competition. In Asia, the most recent countries to adopt market economies — South Korea, Taiwan, Hong Kong, and Singapore — have had dramatic results. Now another group, consisting of Thailand, Malaysia, and Indonesia, is also making gains.

India's nineteen stock markets have been rising faster than any other country's. The economy is reacting to a new policy that, among other things, made the rupee partly convertible, cut import duties, and allowed foreign pension funds to invest in Indian shares. This is a complete turnaround for a country that spent decades discouraging and avoiding foreign trade and investment.

With the opening of European borders to form a single market, products and services from one country are penetrating all the others. In this area, U.S. firms are reaping the benefit. For Digital Equipment, it means greater flexibility to move merchandise between countries. For food companies such as Kraft, it means eliminating the risk that perishable foods will be held up for days waiting for customs clearance. Eastman Kodak can save time and money by adopting uniform packaging. America's economic globalization is creating career opportunities around the world. The difficulty of launching and selling new products is rapidly diminishing. People, goods, services, and capital are able to move more freely between foreign countries and the United States. New regulations allow a bank licensed in one country of an eighteen-member bloc to set up branches anywhere else within those countries.

American blue jeans, cigarettes, and soft drinks are in wide demand internationally. Eastern Europe alone has a population of over 300 million, a huge market in its own right for goods and services, one that has barely been touched and whose potential is just being recognized by western firms. Levi's are being sold in Poland. Pepsi is investing $1 billion in Spain over the next five years to build plants, fast-food restaurants, and a distribution system. Coca-Cola earns 80 percent of its revenues from selling Coke, Sprite, and Fanta overseas, according to *The New York Times* of November 10, 1991. Coors Brewing is forming a joint venture with Jinro, Korea's largest producer of alcoholic beverages, to build a 1.8-million-barrel brewery in Seoul to produce Coors beer. Even specialty stores such as Computerland and Brooks Brothers are operating in Japan. The Colgate-Palmolive Company has an astounding 40 percent of Thailand's shampoo market. America's largest toy retailer, Toys R Us, went international in 1984, first in Canada, then Europe, Hong Kong, Singapore, and now Japan.

Du Pont is investing $2 billion in an aggressive program to expand product distribution in Asia. Apple Computer has connections with more than a hundred Asian software developers. Pizza Hut, Incorporated, Sheraton and Hyatt hotels, and Holiday Inn are signing up franchises and hotel management contracts in the Far East. Citibank is offering automated banking, credit cards, and home-equity loans. On November 11, 1991, *Business Week* reported that Motorola had a $400-million Silicon Harbor complex in Hong Kong and was competing with Japan in every aspect of the telecom and semiconductor markets.

Domino's Pizza is trying to become established in China, where such products as Parker pens, Barbie dolls, and Avon cosmetics (first-year sales, $5 million) are already selling briskly. Haagen-Dazs, founded thirty years ago in the Bronx, New York, is another hot American export with sales in Asia that have doubled to $120 million since 1989.

Asia has a potential television audience of more than 2 billion viewers for programming and advertising. Turner Broadcasting's CNN and ESPN are currently negotiating to enable transmission via satellite systems. MTV Asia was launched in September 1991. That at least partially explains why two of the hottest bootleg items in the People's Republic of China are Madonna videos and Marlboro cigarettes.

Each week 300,000 people rush to experience Japan's Disneyland, outside Tokyo. Euro-Disneyland, a 4,900-acre complex twenty miles east of Paris, promises thirty thousand new jobs by the year 2000. In South American countries, up to 70 percent of the songs played on the radio are in English.

The prices of electronics have dropped steadily while quality and performance have increased. As smaller satellite dishes start appearing and more signals become available, mass distribution should open up individual households to the same number of viewing choices available in the United States. These TVs will create tremendous demand for products and more-sophisticated services, including video technology. Americans and Europeans have proved to be insatiable consumers of music and movies, so imagine the explosion when millions of consumers in India, Africa, and South America have access to videos, CDs, and computer games *and* feel compelled to catch up on sixty years of entertainment!

And here's more encouraging news: It's not even necessary to speak a language other than English to have a business arrangement abroad. Most business-people and vendors understand or are learning English. Furthermore, most trade with the United States is transacted in dollars.

What ventures might work? Selling American books or magazines to a distributor in another country, importing apparel for sale in the United States, arranging trips to the States, or setting up mail-order houses—all of these are possibilities. Almost anything that's popular here can be sold *somewhere*, as long as there is already a demand for the product or service, or if you can create one. Many citizens of other countries will soon be celebrating Valentine's Day for the first time. They don't know it yet, but they need cards, chocolate hearts, and plastic cupids.

There will definitely be more hassles and government red tape involved than you would encounter by hanging your shingle out on Main Street, U.S.A., but then the profit potential is much greater, too.

3

Being a Career Entrepreneur

Combining Your Life with Your Work

As the world changes, old problems endure and new ones evolve, continuously broadening the scope of entrepreneurship.

Since the advent of high technology and computers, we're no longer confined by our skills—just as countries are no longer limited by their resources. It's no longer enough to go to work every day and perform the tasks that someone has laid out for you. A person graduating from high school or college in this decade will most likely have at least three or four *careers* in his or her lifetime—not just jobs, which amount to doing the same thing for different employers.

In this new age, we must integrate all the thoughts, experiences, and challenges of our personal life with our job or business. In essence, we must all be entrepreneurs, constantly striving to offer something new or an improvement on an existing product or service. *Knowing* things has become more important than *making* things. We can now train unskilled cheap labor or produce robots to make things. The key is to come up with the innovations, and to have the know-how to implement them.

Remember, great ideas don't just appear out of the sky like lightning bolts; they come from your storehouse of information, prompted by external stimuli. Therefore, if you keep adding to the storehouse, almost any situation can start a good idea rolling: an untidy desk, children playing, a stroll through the mall, an hour at the laundromat, an irritating phone call aimed at selling you something. However, the most common arena to come up with an innovation is in your present job—even if that's only been flipping burgers, baby-sitting, or pumping gas.

What Is a Career Entrepreneur?

The classic example of an entrepreneur is someone who develops and sells products or services to solve problems that affect a significant number of people. This type of person is constantly examining situations, products, and people's changing needs to find a new opportunity.

Being an entrepreneur, however, does not necessarily mean having an idea, patenting it, drawing up a business plan, and going out to raise venture capital. On a smaller scale, it means finding a better way of doing something—a small innovation. Therefore, your career opportunities lie in generating and exploiting new ideas and solving old problems, whether you work for a company or do it for yourself.

A career entrepreneur doesn't have to be a founder or partner in an organization, or even very high in rank. He or she can be the person unloading the trucks, answering the phones, repairing the equipment, or operating a cash register. The difference between the career entrepreneur and the person who will be a career cashier is *observation* and *action*. The career entrepreneur is constantly searching for better ways to do things and taking the initiative to implement them.

By being an innovator instead of just a worker,

you can be a career entrepreneur and work in the same field, business, or company your entire life. It's not necessary to start your own business; you can be an entrepreneur within the structure of a corporation. (This is sometimes called "intrapreneurship.") Career entrepreneurship is about doing your best work and really using your skills, talents, and powers of observation in whatever you're doing.

If you, the career entrepreneur, have a truly novel concept or product, you will work out the details and present them to your company. If the company is receptive, position yourself as a part of their developing your innovation. If it turns out that the company isn't interested in the concept, or that someone else has already come up with it in some form, stepping forward will help you make valuable contacts or even earn you a degree of visibility. However, if you cannot advance your idea on the inside, yet still feel that it is viable, you may want to consider taking it somewhere else.

You may be saying to yourself, "I'm no genius. Sure, I'm ambitious, but I want to find and stay with something solid, where the money is, not constantly be running around." Well, let me repeat that it's no longer realistic to plan on settling in until retirement; society and the economy are in such flux that the only "security" is in moving around *with* the money and being ready to retool with new skills, based on a solid general education! (One thing I learned on Wall Street was that money doesn't disappear, it merely changes hands.) You have to keep *ahead* of the game, or pretty soon you're not even playing! You can't afford to set yourself up as a virtual victim, like so many in the early nineties who've found themselves suddenly laid off or seen their entire industry or profession become obsolete. So a certain degree of entrepreneurship *is* a necessity if you wish to flourish in today's marketplace.

The recent oversupply of M.B.A. graduates provides another good example of why you must look insightfully toward the future instead of jumping on today's bandwagon. At one time, having an M.B.A. set you apart from the crowd; today it's commonplace and therefore less meaningful. The January 20, 1992, edition of *Forbes* reported that in 1962 only 6 percent of all master's degrees awarded in the United States were in business administration. Twenty years later, 25 percent were—hardly a way to distinguish yourself.

Just fifteen years ago, high school students were warned about the glut in the teacher's market and told that it was career suicide to major in education. Now there is a shortage of teachers, and practically anyone with a degree has a job waiting, especially in declining urban areas. A science teacher has real negotiating clout. And in some states, such as New Jersey, people with subject knowledge who don't even have teaching degrees are happily being recruited. Remember that fads and trends occur as much in education as they do in clothing and politics. Doing what's hot this month isn't about thinking, it's *reacting*. Step back a little and consider the bigger picture.

How to Start Thinking Like a Career Entrepreneur

Being a career entrepreneur isn't necessarily arduous. It can even *be fun*. It just takes practice until it becomes a habit. The main elements involved are *observation, vision,* and, most of all, *common sense*. People with vision often become great artists, statesmen, musicians, and writers. In business, having vision means creating the next Coca-Cola, Levi's, Home-Shopping Network, or basically anything we've seen in the *Back to the Future* movie trilogy.

Ted Turner is a perfect example of a visionary businessperson. The creator of CNN and TBS was one of the first media moguls to see the possibilities of cable television. (Old-movie colorization didn't work out so well; even forward-thinking entrepreneurs can make bad judgment calls.) Vision is great if you have it, but you don't need it to succeed. What you need is *common sense.*

Common sense means deciding to take an umbrella because you look out your window and it's raining, not because the television weatherman said there was a 50-percent chance of showers. Some of the most successful businesses ever launched were based on common sense and often on simple observations. Philip Knight, once a mile runner for the University of Oregon, came up with the concept of marketing a high-quality recreational shoe to professional athletes at a lower price. So he founded Nike. He even took his perception a bit further. Aware of the American public's cultlike devotion to its heroes, Knight reasoned that the sneakers professional athletes wore would be emulated by the masses. He also figured that if men could be persuaded to wear flower-power pendants, long hair, and Nehru jackets because the Beatles did it, there was untold potential in selling something trendy that was also a basic necessity!

Back in 1972, when he began, Knight forsaw the trend toward health consciousness and physical fitness, and the sneaker's status as a truly American apparel staple—both of which allowed him to position Nike products for success. He was right—in the 1960s you were only allowed to wear sneakers for gym or after-school play. As school dress codes loosened, slowly Nikes became part of the shoe mainstream. Nowadays it's not uncommon to see a seventy-year-old grandmother show up at a Broadway theater all decked out in her best Castlebury suit and pearls with a pair of high-top Reeboks under her skirt. Today Knight is rich, and all because he had a simple, good idea literally right at his feet.

More recently, while many retail giants have been falling into Chapter 11, Nancy Ganz, thirty-six, is making millions with body-slimming clothes. Her flagship product, the Hipslip, which is a nineties version of the old-fashioned girdle, debuted at Bloomingdale's in November 1987. Ganz capitalized on a fashion trend popularized by Madonna, who began wearing undergarments as outer garments.

Simple common sense is abundant and free; it doesn't come from books but from observation. For example, a businessman friend of mine decided to purchase a diner in New York City. Uneducated in the traditional sense, but street-smart after years of working in Manhattan restaurants, he paid little heed to records he was shown for six possible diners he was considering. Knowing full well that the books were probably doctored to enable the sellers to increase the diners' price, the restaurateur drove around the city at 5:00 A.M. (just before the street-cleaners arrived) at least ten times over a one-month period, stopping to scrutinize the amount of garbage on the sidewalks and streets in front of all of his potential businesses. Assuming that the biggest moneymaker would be frequented by the greatest number of customers, he ended up buying the diner *with the most litter in front of it.* Obviously, that was where the most people passed by. That was almost a decade ago, and not only is Jack and Jill's Diner in Manhattan's Greenwich Village still well patronized, but the owner was recently able to install substantial renovations.

Predicting what will happen to the economy is a difficult task to which there are several approaches, most involving more common sense than scientific method. Sure, highly acclaimed economists study the interest rate markets, budget deficit, unemployment figures, new housing starts, etc., to make their predictions for articles in *The Wall Street Journal*. But often it seems that they would have been better off doing some simple field work. Try making some of your own business observations:

• Go to the local mall on Saturday and see how many shopping bags customers are carrying. Are they spending or just looking?

• See how your local used-car dealer is doing. If he's having a stellar month, the economy probably isn't, or people would be buying *new* cars.

• Ask a friend who works in retail if the store has experienced a lot of theft this month. The five-finger discount—also known as stolen goods, or what stores politely refer to as shrinkage—skyrockets during rough economic times.

• Are people frequenting restaurants at mealtime? Or are they feeling cost-conscious and taking the extra time to shop and cook at home? Eating out is usually the first cut when the paycheck needs to be stretched and likewise the first activity to be resumed when there's a little cash left over.

• Is everyone licking Haagen-Dazs bars? When consumer spending is falling, ice cream consumption mysteriously rises. It seems that small, inexpensive treats like hot fudge sundaes are a consolation when we can't easily afford big-ticket items.

In general, making astute business observations means constantly being on the lookout for trends and new ideas and, most important, searching for ways to improve upon *existing* structures. Use common sense to determine what areas are becoming obsolete and which will be growing.

What Fields and Companies Should You Examine?

Search for fields and companies in which you have a specific interest and that address problems in innovative ways that are likely to be popular. If you're already studying for a particular career, observe what may apply to it.

If you're mechanically inclined and that's where your interests lie, some areas to observe may be snow removal, home construction and repair, motors, appliances, and car repair and resale markets. Many repair and service shops have grown from one person into major businesses. To many car owners it's worth twenty dollars just to get their oil changed. Also look in the reference section of your library for *Dun's Industrial Guide: The Metalworking Directory*. (For information on these and other works mentioned, see the Resource Guide at the end of the book.) This guide to the manufacturing market in the United States provides data on more than seventy thousand original equipment manufacturers and metal distributors. Maybe you can think of a way that a school, business, or government organization in your area can make better use of its machinery and production techniques in order to save time and money.

If you have had a good experience in selling consumer goods and enjoy it, then observe these areas: cosmetics, food products, car dealerships, street fairs, flea markets, fast foods, and department stores. Glance through the *Directory of United States Importers* to see if there is a product that should be made available in your area.

Learning about services is a great inroad to acquiring the on-the-job training and knowledge for promotions. For instance, if haircutting is your thing, after being a hair stylist you may eventually want to start your own shop or perhaps work for a movie or television studio. If you install air conditioners, you may eventually hire people to work for you. If you're interested in service, start by observing these areas: restaurants and hotels, catering, gardening, teaching (at camps or retirement community centers if you don't have a degree), lawn maintenance, cleaning (of cars, homes, businesses, boats, clothes, windows, and basements), care-giving (babies, older people, sick people, or pets), shopping for others (and businesses), or cooking (for colleges, restaurants, private homes, clubs, camps, or hospitals).

If you're the creative type, then observe acting, working in stage productions, sewing, drawing, designing ads and posters, and photography. If you're interested in culture, art, music, dance, or theater you should definitely read *Careers for Culture Lovers and Other Artsy Types*, by Marjorie Eberts and Margaret Gisler. This book contains information about occupations such as choreography, art restoration, antiquarian bookselling, arts management, curatorship, wardrobing, and technicians.

For information on starting your own business, expanding what your company does, or just in some way enhancing your present job, jump-start your creativity by reading magazines such as *Successful Home Business, Small Business Opportunities, Entrepreneur, New Business Opportunities*, and *D&B Reports for Small Business Management*. You don't have to plan on becoming an entrepreneur just to look at these magazines for some fresh ideas. *Entrepreneurial Woman* magazine contains a list of hot new business ideas, including organizational consulting, computer education for children, and utility bill auditing. Every suggestion, as with most "idea" magazines, gives plenty of information on how things work, how to get involved, licensing, partnerships, insurance costs, etc. *The Small Business Development Catalog,* published by the Entrepreneur Group, sells more than 165 guides with ideas for businesses you can run from home, start in your spare time, and begin with little investment.

Trend analysis is another useful tool in examining the areas that interest you to find out what might be "hot." Marketing wizard Faith Popcorn's 1991 book, *The Popcorn Report,* does just that. In it she predicts upcoming trends such as the following:

• Day spas: relaxing mini-retreats costing only about seven dollars or eight dollars, for people who can't pay $3,500 a week, or just don't have the time to get away.

• Customized shoes and jeans tailored for individuals through laser measuring and computer layout, and constructed by robots.

• More people working at home or going a step further and "cashing out" by leaving the executive life to do such things as start a dairy in the country or work for a social-action group.

• A continued increase in "small indulgence" products, such as designer fountain pens, fancy lingerie, and roses—luxurious little things that pick you up when new clothes or vacations are too costly.

For more ideas read *American Demographics* monthly magazine, which lists new consumer trends, and see if any of your product ideas can be tailored to match up with what's in demand. Here are some of the trends the magazine lists that might spark some of your own observations and ideas:

• The United States has almost as many pets as people. Feeding, pampering, doctoring, and burying them is a multibillion-dollar industry that will continue to grow. Vets who are willing to make house calls are in demand.

• Vacation property will boom in the 90's. The decline of the nation's cities is putting a weekend getaway on the top of most families' "want" list ahead of actual vacations.

• Strong consumer demand for toys from the 1950s and 1960s has created a recession-proof market for these items.

American Demographics also gives information about which consumer groups have extra money, how to make the perfect mailing list, how to target older Americans, and how to create attractive labeling.

However, it's not enough only to realize that change creates opportunities. You have to identify the changes and where they could lead. Determining what people will be doing, wearing, and thinking so that we can serve them is something anyone can do. It simply means observing friends, family, neighbors, and people on the street. What transportation are they using? Bikes, rollerblades, cars? If so, what models or brands? What are they wearing? Manhattan wholesale clothing supplier Adam Cohen says that almost all clothing trends can be spotted walking out of thrift stores almost a year before they become mainstream. What are people protesting in front of Town Hall? Why are you being asked to sign a petition at the entrance to the supermarket? What television shows do your parents watch? What gadgets or magazines do your friends, brothers, and sisters enjoy?

More important, what do people *believe*? Not necessarily in a religious sense, but what do they want for the future? Recently at a barbecue I saw a five-year-old insist his dad was destroying the environment by spritzing water on the hot grill. If a five-year-old is worried about something, there is a good chance it's an issue that a lot of other people will care about—if not now, definitely in the future.

Talk to sales clerks and find out what's selling and why. Go to the park and see what type of exercising is popular and who's doing it. If you're really brave, find some teenagers and ask them what type of music they like and what they do when not in school. Ask people what type of conveniences would make their lives easier.

Go about your daily routine and think about how it's changed since you were a kid, and what larger trends these changes imply. Stroll the mall and enter a boutique or restaurant. In the seventies, a popular sign and salesperson's refrain was "No substitutions, no exchanges, and no refunds." That sign isn't on the wall anymore. As more companies are being forced to compete for business, they are finally realizing they must *serve* their customers instead of ringing the register and running.

Think of the long-distance services Sprint and MCI. Phone service is a good example of a business that once required the consumer to approach the company (frequently with fingers crossed); now the phone company aggressively markets and advertises to lure customers. You don't *have* to use AT&T long distance anymore, so now they must give you a reason to stay. Most phone businesses now offer everything from no-charge trial periods to free service if anything goes wrong. Did the receptionist at the dentist's office make a goodwill phone call to your home the day after you got a cavity filled? Sure—it's worth it to them. If you're not happy, there are dozens of other dentists in the phone book. The individual who came up with the national referral service "1-800-DENTIST" knew that, too.

Continue your mall walk and visit the fast-food joint or department store. Notice that good service has come to mean personalization, immortalized in the Burger King slogan, "Have It Your Way!" Chains such as Wendy's and Sizzler offer make-it-yourself salad bars or sundae bars. Computers stationed in malls let kids create their own storybooks with their names and the names of their friends and pets inside. Music stores provide facilities that allow you to create your own mixed tapes. Actress Meg Ryan as Sally in the movie *When Harry Met Sally* summed up this trend best. Harry (Billy Crystal) was astounded by her complicated food orders, which usually ended up with half of the stuff "on the side," and he demanded to know why she always had to make so many special requests. Sally simply replied, "I want it the way I want it." Add to that, "when I want it," and you have today's consumer. Instant gratification is not something one forgoes after becoming accustomed to it. Successful people, products, and services are going to continue to offer accessibility and individuality.

Now take a trip over to the newsstand. To use common sense in predicting what type of jobs will be created, you must study the problems the nation and the world are currently facing. Do this by reading the newspapers, listening to politicians' campaign points, checking weekly news magazines, and watching informational television shows such as "60 Minutes." Opportunities lie in the solutions to or management of those problems.

If you'd looked at the national edition of *The New York Times* (a paper available even on the windswept plains of Minot, North Dakota) on December 17, 1991, for example, you'd have found some important information in a headline on the front page: "Russia Needs Managers." It goes on to say that a growing Russian economy, with markets open to western trade and employment, will stimulate western economies. The best way we can help Russia is to send American managers and consultants to the large plants and banks there, and to assist small business people. If you have any sort of management expertise, this could mean the start of a fascinating lifetime of work for you. One might begin by calling the consulting firms mentioned in the article and exploring employment with them.

Closer to home was this lead story in *The New York Times* on February 9, 1992: "Crime and Its Amplified Echoes Are Rearranging People's Lives." It focused on increasing rates of murder, sexual assault, and "Rolex robberies." Look at the other side of this article to find what opportunities it suggests. Also consider the number of "real life" television shows that re-create crimes (like "America's Most Wanted"); the televised rape trials of William Kennedy Smith and boxer Mike Tyson; even the way George Bush used convict Willie Horton in his 1988 presidential campaign. What can you conclude? People are obsessed with crime!

No matter what happens to the crime rate over the next few years, security needs are going way up — everything from home and car fortifications such as alarm systems, steering-wheel bar locks, and light timers to security guards, parking-lot lights, and self-defense and gun-training classes. These products and systems have to be designed, manufactured, marketed, distributed, and serviced, or taught to others, and that means more jobs and businesses.

The science section of the newspaper is especially important, as it documents current problems, dangerous situations, and crises. Newspapers raise questions such as "Can technology solve traffic jams?" and "Is experimenting on lab animals necessary?" Today's concerns are the basis for tomorrow's solutions, and will require entire industries dedicated to them: infertility, childhood lead poisoning, chemical waste, radon, immunization, crop irrigation, drought, AIDS, and so on.

To learn still more about important trends and issues, go to the magazine sections of libraries and bookstores. Virtually every type of occupation has some sort of trade magazine or industry newsletter, where you can learn of the hottest issues, trends, and problems that people in specific fields are working to solve. A list of all trade magazines can be found in the library reference books *Magazines for Libraries*, by Bill Katz and Linda Sternberg Katz, and *Ulrich's International Periodicals Directory*, which is updated annually. *Newsletters in Print* is a guide to more than 10,300 subscription, membership, and free newsletters, bulletins, and digests in the United States and Canada. When studying your magazines, pay special attention to ads, the classified section, reviews of other literature, and announcements of upcoming trade shows or events.

If you aren't yet ready for specifics, then check *Time, Newsweek, The Wall Street Journal, The Economist,* and *Business Week* as well as computer, health, and science publications, and even *People* to get a knowledge of new products, consumer trends, technology, and the industries that are thriving and the ones that are facing crisis. Even that checkout-line barometer of public taste, *The National Enquirer,* is recommended study for determining what's on people's minds.

Popular entertainment media also embrace topics of current interest. Yes—even if you're a couch potato, you can be using that "veg-out" time to observe and plan for your career. Talk shows and made-for-TV movies try to feature every crisis, concern, and conflict *du jour* along with who's hot and who's not. Song lyrics are topical, if not occasionally prophetic, while the accompanying videos contain all the latest fashions and gimmicks. Even prime-time sitcoms have been focusing on issues such as drug abuse and teen sex, making "The Partridge Family" look like something out of the Victorian era instead of two decades ago.

Another thing to watch is advertisements. It's good to keep track of which companies and individuals are marketing what products and services. If something is new or doing well, the marketing is usually stepped up. For example, you'll hear commercials for the product on the radio, see billboards and magazine spreads, perhaps receive a reduced-price coupon or a sample, and maybe even catch Ed McMahon or Tony Randall pitching it on TV. *The Information Catalog* contains industry and market reports, research from Wall Street company reports, and a directory of source books for more than thirty-eight industries.

In your observations, take note of any recent fads. Such crazes as those for Cabbage Patch Kids, "slap bracelets," Rubik's Cube, and mood rings are great if you're the one who thought them up or bought the rights and marketed them. Even better are enduring fads such as skateboarding and rollerblading. These have offshoots that include new designs, clubs, competitions, magazines, safety gear, events, and accessories. Novelties themselves, though they change rapidly (remember the Super Ball? trolls? pet rocks?), are forever popular — as whoever started the Wham-O company realized. No matter how absurd your idea seems, remind yourself that people are willing to pay good money for diamond-shaped yellow signs imprinted GRANDMA ON BOARD, which adhere to the inside of a car window.

For some people, starting their own business is the only way to go. If that's your inclination then you have lots of research to do. Get a book such as *Your Small Business Made Simple*, by Richard R. Gallagher, to understand planning, financing, and developing your product or service, finding the right market for it and merchandising it, and so on. You will need another book that gives specific information on writing business contracts, incorporating, paying taxes, and hiring employees. Depending on whether you want to raise capital from friends, family, or a bank loan, it might also be necessary to draw up a business plan. Also investigate *The Franchise Opportunities Guide* for a list of existing businesses that can be purchased and operated by individual owners who are willing to follow a prescribed formula.

If you've ever embarked on some type of self-employment, then you've already been thinking like an entrepreneur. Here are some examples of entrepreneurial ventures that require extremely low overhead and are very straightforward. People often set them up as full-scale businesses or part-time jobs, or just to earn extra cash.

- Gift basket service
- Videotaping service
- Christmas tree sales
- Flower vending
- Home remodeling
- Driveway sealing
- Pet grooming
- Tutoring planning
- Recycling program consulting
- Chimney sweeping
- Pool service
- Personal shopping
- Seminar promoting
- Catering
- Resumé writing
- Bicycle tour planning
- Auto painting
- Herb farming
- Telephone information service (900 number) for weather, sports, news, etc.

Students at Regis College in Denver, Colorado, are busy with a profitable twenty-four-hour condom-delivery service to dorm rooms. They charge $1.50 per prophylactic (a markup from the store price) and—let's face it—are providing a public service.

As you can see, searching for needs to fill is not a matter of gazing into a crystal ball. It's being *observant* that counts. Genius does not consist in knowing things, but in knowing what to look for and where to find information.

4

Seeing Problems as Opportunities

As we've discussed, everywhere you look, issues and changes abound. The career entrepreneur, fascinated by the possibilities, studies these problems and starts asking questions. While stalled in a car or bus on the way to school or the office, he or she looks out the window and muses, "Can technology reduce traffic jams by removing toll booths and electronically scanning cars as they pass, like groceries in a supermarket, and then sending drivers a bill at the end of the month?" "Is it possible to build magnetic levitation rail systems on popular routes such as L.A. to San Francisco and New York to Boston?" "Why does everyone in the world who is changing planes have to go to O'Hare Airport and compete with all the travelers who actually want to go to Chicago? Could these hubs be restructured?"

Let's look at various types of problems and how real entrepreneurs are creating ventures to solve them.

Social Problems

Here are some social problems that have yet to be solved:

Since we put men on the moon in 1969, the price of housing has risen about 500 percent. Isn't there some way to build affordable housing? Why not bring back the Murphy bed for small apartments? Why not facilitate more community living, as there is in Sweden and Israel, to help working parents? One can buy a straightforward book on how to commit suicide and yet adopting children is still so difficult, often resulting in shady dealings. Not having an accessible, well-run adoption market only results in hardship for all parties—the mothers giving up their children, the infants themselves, and the adoptive parents.

Increasingly, business is being used to solve social problems:

• In Bloomington, Minnesota, a suburb of Minneapolis, the school board has approved classrooms for the new $625-million Mall of America, intended to be the nation's biggest shopping center. Children in any of three districts will be eligible to apply three thousand to four thousand dollars in state aid to attend the mall school. Child-care and work study programs for students training in retail trades will also be offered. Most of the participants will probably be children of the ten thousand people scheduled to work there. This arrangement should be ideal for parents trying to spend more time with children or to be on hand for transportation or emergencies. Businesses that lease stores in this mall can count on having a larger selection of well-qualified employees who will be more comfortable about their personal lives and therefore more productive—and who will provide additional patronage for mall stores as these employees purchase what they need for their families.

• Safe sex used to mean knowing what time your parents would be home on bowling night. Now the prevention of sexually transmitted diseases is becoming a specialized and lucrative market, though admittedly the subject is socially and politically charged. Fox Television aired the first network condom ad on November 17, 1991; no doubt condom makers will soon be allowed to advertise their brands on TV. The condom industry's two biggest firms, Carter-Wallace (makers of Trojan) and Britain's London International Group (makers of Durex and Ramses) control 90 percent of the $250-million American market. Some smaller companies are having fun with this serious product to enhance their sales. The store next to my apartment building in New York City was selling condoms in a rainbow of colors, as well as ones that glow in the dark and a kind imprinted with a ruler design so the enthusiastic lover can size himself up.

• New York City's mayor, David Dinkins, is exploring the private sector for a solution to homelessness. One of his committee's recommendations included permitting private, nonprofit service agencies to run the programs for the bureaucratically bogged-down Division of Health and Human Services. Through the new agencies the city would provide job training, psychotherapy, and drug rehabilitation as a prerequisite for obtaining subsidized housing.

Easing Crises
Crisis can often be the stimulus for solving problems. We become fully aware of some problems only by experiencing them personally and dramatically. If you drive to work every day, crowded buses and subway fires aren't something you have a vested interest in researching and attempting to improve. Likewise, people don't normally sit around and discuss how patients could be made more comfortable during a hospital stay unless they themselves or their loved

ones wind up in traction. From the trying experience of dealing with unfortunate circumstances, we better understand the problems and develop a compassion for people undergoing similar discomforts. If you're able to help yourself in a new way, then pass it on.

Here are some lucrative solutions to crises:

• Parker H. Petit launched Healthdyne Incorporated, a company dedicated to manufacturing infant monitoring systems, after his six-month-old son died of Sudden Infant Death Syndrome.

• Cross Creek Recreational Products, Incorporated, got its start as a result of a wife's search for adult puzzles and toys to occupy her husband, whose mind was eroding from Pick's disease (a degenerative disease of the brain, similar to Alzheimer's).

• Around New York City, a new 900-number service provides professional medical advice over the phone for three dollars a minute. How about more such numbers to answer inquiries about personal finances, legalities, pet care, or just simple home repairs? Or 1-900-THERAPY for psychiatric counseling?

• In 1982, Martine Kempf designed a computer program that could be used to operate voice-controlled wheelchairs. In California's Silicon Valley, she set up a factory to manufacture and market her invention. Kempf was inspired by her father, a polio victim, who designed a hand-controlled automobile, and later by armless German teenagers unable to move their wheelchairs.

• Each year, 2.3 million fires are reported in the United States, accounting for more than 6,200 deaths and 100,000 injuries and over $10 billion in property damage. The U.S. Fire Administration (a division of the National Fire Academy) in Emmetsburg, Maryland, has developed several fire prevention kits to help people stay safe. There is a tremendous market in training people — especially children — how to prepare for typical emergencies through videos, practice programs, and easy-to-use equipment.

• The National Institute of Mental Health in Rockville, Maryland, reports that about 12.5 percent of the adult population (22.5 million people) experience some type of phobia at one time or another. When phobias such as the fear of having a heart attack or the fear of dying start interfering with work or your lifestyle, it's time to see a phobia treatment specialist. These centers are appearing as people realize the necessity of treating serious phobias. USAIR's Fearful Flyers Program, a seven-week evening course that includes a visit to an air-traffic control tower, is available at airports in ten major cities. It can even be worthwhile to work on smaller problems such as fear of cats, heights, and snakes. What other physical or mental discomforts would people want to eliminate if it were convenient and affordable?

• Last year's "doll of the year" in Europe was Judy, a Barbie-like figure with a detachable full-term fetus hidden behind her plastic abdomen. Although studies prove it, you don't need to read one to realize that more single working women are choosing to become mothers. This trend is paving the way for every type of family support network imaginable, from services that organize transportation to medical appointments, shopping, childcare, and the need for fast, healthy meals.

• As families feel the pressure to bolster their incomes, it's not uncommon for a husband and wife to have full-time jobs and the teenage children in a household to have part-time jobs. Often this creates a problem if there are older people in the home who don't belong in a total-care facility, but do need daily attention. Affordable senior day-care centers are appearing across the nation just as child day care became popular two decades ago as more mothers went back to work.

Filling Lacks

Maybe there is a service or product you would like, but it is not currently available in an appropriate or accessible form. Chances are, many other people would probably like the same thing. Countless businesses have been launched on this assumption: diet programs, fitness ventures, dating services, book clubs, biking groups, day camps, special-interest magazines, community music groups, newsletters, specialty boutiques, clothing stores specializing in irregular sizes, frozen yogurt stands, and singing telegrams, to name but a few. Think about it — certainly the inventor of the school bus was once a mortified kid fed up with being driven to school by a mother wearing a pink fuzzy bathrobe, wedgie slippers, a beauty mask, and curlers, with a smoke dangling from her unglossed lips.

It's also common to notice that existing products are adequate, but what's currently available isn't completely satisfactory. Good examples can be found in the slight modifications people have made on their own, and which are then adopted and improved upon by a manufacturer. For example, people have always improvised ways to fight the elements. L. L. Bean, the founder of the pioneering mail-order company, developed rubber-soled hunting shoes after walking around a campfire with socks and rubbers on his feet. In the 1970s, Americans got tired of coming in out of the sun to the shade of their cars in the summertime, only to have to sit down on scorching hot plastic. Some motorists even kept towels in their cars to cover the seats. Since then, auto manufacturers have begun to use materials that retain less heat, and retailers are selling countless carboard window shields, many decorated with pictures or humorous phrases.

Fast-food chains picked up on their customers' at-home habit of putting their bacon and eggs between two slices of toast. They now offer them the same thing in seconds, in the form of all styles of breakfast sandwiches—generations removed from the original Egg McMuffin—conveniently packaged for eating on the road.

There are plenty of other situations that spark innovations:

War

During both world wars, the greatest advances in science and technology were made as nations scrambled to gain military advantage by building more effective and efficient weaponry, communications equipment, and other war materials. These mechanical improvements were later transferred to industry. Medical advances have also flourished during wartime. For example, great strides were made in plastic surgery during World War II, a war that also fueled the race to develop penicillin.

Entertainment

Risky Business, the 1983 hit film, sparked a desire for Ray-Ban sunglasses just as *Top Gun*, the box-office success about fighter pilots, ignited a demand for repro-bomber jackets. Nick at Nite, the cable television station that airs sitcoms from the fifties, sixties, and seventies, helps fuel the resurgence of popularity in art-deco diners, canvas sneakers, and bowling shirts.

America's appetite for standup comedy went from live shows, such as those popularized by the Catskill resorts in the fifties, to television variety shows hosted by such personalities as Ed Sullivan and Milton Berle. Then standup comedy spawned nightclubs across the country. Television specials followed, featuring comics like Richard Pryor, Robin Williams, and George Carlin, to name but a few. And now comedy has landed its very own TV network, Comedy Central.

Convenience

Paradoxically, laziness or impatience prompts some people to labor long hours to devise things that will permanently make their lives easier. No one enjoyed having to get up to change channels; hence someone developed remote control. Not wanting to wait for food to cook resulted in the development of the microwave oven. Overhead dryers for hair were awkward and slow, so the blow-dryer and curling iron were introduced. The practice of sticking notes to walls, desks, and briefcases with Scotch tape led to the Post-it note. The Post-it, by the way, was discovered by accident. A scientist was trying to develop a super-duper glue, and so far had only come up with a temporary adhesive; it stuck, but could be pulled up again easily. Instead of being frustrated, 3M, the company the scientist worked for, invented Post-it notes and cornered a market. (Serendipity is also the mother of invention—and of careers.)

Hiring a professional wedding planner used to be a luxury in which only the wealthy could afford to indulge. However, as more couples find themselves working long hours to save money for things their parents could afford with a single income, a new market is emerging in the form of wedding planning for the not so rich or famous. It seems to be worth a week's salary to take the aggravation out of saying "I do." Instead of agonizing over decorations and hors d'oeuvres for months in advance, the betrothed can simply call their own answering machines to find a message from the wedding planner, who's done it all for them.

Play

Child's play has led to the creation of many consumer pleasures. In 1959, Ruth Handler, a vice-president of Mattel, Incorporated, came up with a product that brought the company international fame and quadrupled sales: the Barbie doll. Handler got her idea to create a grown-up doll when she noticed her young daughter, after whom Barbie is named, bypassing dolls her own age for teenage dolls with fashion accessories. Until that time, the only such dolls were paper cutouts.

Retailers of the popular long-range super-squirt gun that is marketed to kids have recently been surprised to find that a large number of their customers are college students and working adults.

Affinity

Look to your own community or group for problems that need solving. Some examples are regional issues, or problems of women and minorities. Even a personal trait can be a useful catalyst for business ideas. For example, every five years there seems to be a "lefty" rebellion. Stores and catalogs offer items such as scissors and can openers designed for left-handed users. Meanwhile, newspapers and talk shows make much of studies on whether lefties are smarter, stupider, wackier, or just more eccentric than righties.

When the teetotalers started outnumbering the

drinkers at some local water holes, juice bars became popular. Friends could still enjoy the nightlife with nonalcoholic beverages without worrying about appointing a designated driver.

PBS's "Scientific American Frontiers" portrayed a quadriplegic marathoner who wanted more mobility. He designed a streamlined, user-friendly wheelchair, suitable for physically challenged athletes like himself, and now produces and markets these chairs to others as a business.

Women now make up 49 percent of new-car purchases and designer Mimi Vandermolen at Ford Motor Co. has taken the needs of women drivers into account. She has introduced a lighter weight trunk door and a lowered front end, to give shorter women a better view of the road. Her next projects involve eliminating seat buttons that entangle skirts and rip panty hose along with bulky gas and brake pedals that make driving difficult for women wearing high heels.

Obsolescence

Be the first one to notice that a traditional service is still in demand and then improve on methods that have become inefficient or outdated. For instance, Mail Boxes Etc. is a franchise that offers wrapping, packing, and shipping to those who don't have the materials handy and don't have the time or the courage to stand in line at the post office. Franchise owners blatantly charge 30 percent more for stamps, UPS, and Federal Express, taking full advantage of a frenetic society willing to pay extra for convenience. It's air-conditioned, you don't have to wait in line, and to date there haven't been any shooting sprees by disgruntled ex-employees.

Businesses have always needed signs to announce

themselves, whether neon, electronic, or plain black and white. Instant signage services that don't require a three-week wait are getting more and more business.

Creating a Need

With all the genuine needs out there, you'd think there would be no need to create any. But sometimes the solution comes *before* the problem. Henry Ford first marketed his automobile to farmers and created the demand by producing the right machine at a reasonable price. It wasn't until almost a decade later, when enough people started moving to the suburbs and continued working in cities, that cars became a necessity for commuters and enabled many more families to change their lifestyles.

Akio Morita of the Sony Corporation has constantly created needs with electronic products such as pocket radios, digital cameras, and the Walkman. Somehow we all used to exist just fine without remote-control answering machines and VCRs. Now they seem an indispensable part of the furnishings and accessories we not only expect to have, but *insist* upon having, in our homes.

The dreaded Christmas fruitcake is spilling over into everyday consumption. Specialty bread stores are opening the market for croissants of many different flavors, as well as bread made from oats, bran, and wheat combined with fruits, and many other variations on the traditional loaf.

Luxury goods are another example of items people don't really need, but will work toward acquiring. An upscale store, The Sharper Image, has aligned itself with distribution of such products, including specialized workout equipment, high-tech sunglasses, and baby strollers designed so the operator can wear rollerblades.

By training yourself to be more observant, you can really enhance your career prospects, whether you find a new way of manufacturing, a way to help people with a specific problem, or just a way to save a few steps in office drudgery. If your first few ideas aren't viable (e.g., frozen toast), sooner or later something will come along. Remember that Silly Putty was originally leftover chemical waste. That's why the package warns you not to eat it. And contrary to the myth promulgated on a television commercial by Bill Cosby, Jell-O does not grow on trees. Discovered by the nineteenth-century industrialist Peter Cooper, gelatin was originally a by-product of assembly-line slaughter and packing operations. Fortunately, before the new product was perfected and marketed, Mrs. Cooper had the good sense to add some flavoring.

PART II

A Step-by-Step Plan for Career
Development

5

What to Do with Your Life If You Decide Not to Join the Army

The army claims that it does more before 9:00 A.M. than the rest of us do all day. I think that's great and I appreciate the job they do, but this slogan is just *not* a big incentive for me. By nine, I haven't had three cups of coffee, watched cartoons, or even checked my horoscope. What works well for some people isn't always the answer for others.

The navy, on the other hand, once had a great slogan: "Join the Navy and see the world." This is much more appealing to me (although I have a suspicion that they also do a lot before nine). So if you can't see the world, knowing as much as you can about it, as we discussed in the first two chapters, is definitely important. But being aware of your surroundings is only part of it. If you don't know who *you* are, what your abilities are, and what you want from life, you're going to make more mistakes than necessary.

A career entrepreneur is a self-aware person, perhaps one with a dream, but certainly one with ability. You're an individual and not a clone. It's time to zero in on your personality and skills in order to use them to your utmost advantage.

The time to get into the right career is now. Because the longer you wait, the easier it is to get comfortable and lose the faith and courage necessary to try something new or get into an area where you'll need lots of training or studying. Fear of failure keeps most people at a job that's drudgery, wondering if they could have succeeded at something they would have really enjoyed—managing a rock band, working for the FBI, producing movies, or decorating cakes—whatever their interest is!

Finding Your True Calling

1. Go to the biggest bookstore in your area. If you live in the country or a small town, go to the nearest city. Spend a few hours browsing. What subjects do you gravitate toward? What would you read about if you had all the free time in the world? Make a list of these subjects, even if some are very obscure, such as string art, retina surgery, or very traditional hobbies like stamp collecting or toy making.

2. Visit the nearest library that has a good reference section. Try to get a research pass to use the local college or university library, if there is one. For the truly undecided, the *Dictionary of Occupational Titles* lists almost one thousand jobs by category along with a brief description of each. The U.S. Department of Labor publishes an annual prognosis for the job market titled *The Occupational Outlook Handbook*, which is also available in the library. It contains a summary of what tomorrow's job market is projected to be like, along with descriptions of hundreds of different occupations. Each profile contains an analysis of what type of working conditions to expect, employment outlook for that field, necessary training and qualifications, possibilities for advancement, potential earnings, related occupations, and sources of additional information.

3. Another useful government publication is the *The Occupational Outlook Quarterly*. It contains an overview of the economy, with a forecast of employment projections for about 250 occupations. The thirty fastest-growing occupations and fields with the greatest job growth are also highlighted.

4. Go to the biggest magazine store in town or the closest city. List the ten magazines you would get regularly if subscriptions were free. Again, scan the periodical and newsletter directory in the library and send away for additional materials that may be of interest. Some publishers will even send a sample copy or let you purchase one copy before committing yourself to buying a subscription. Magazines are indispensable because they contain information on the most up-to-date technologies and innovations, as well as profiles of new companies and extraordinary people, along with specific advertisements and classified ads.

5. What section of the newspaper do you read first? Politics, travel, entertainment, sports, comics? If sports is your true love, look in the career section of the bookstore for *Career Opportunities in the Sports Industry*, by Shelly Field. Maybe you should manage a team or handle publicity, or perhaps you should be a sportscaster, operate the scoreboard, or test the AstroTurf.

If the travel section is all you want, maybe you should read *How to Get a Job with a Cruise Line*, by Mary Fallon Miller. The Love Boat may have a place for you!

6. Review all of your hobbies and activities. What do you do in your spare time? Or better yet, what do you do when you *should* be studying for a math test or mowing the lawn? If the answer is ride

horses, build model airplanes, or sky-dive, then maybe this, as opposed to your major in school, is a starting point to look for a career. The House of Collectibles series of books by Random House offers price guides and directories for such items as antiques, beer cans, toys, cars, *Star Trek* and *Star Wars* collectibles, comic books, baseball and football cards, and dolls, among other things.

7. Make a list of your skills and qualities in order to determine a compatible field. For example, skills you have may include analyzing data, coordinating events, displaying artistic ideas, listening to others, or bookkeeping. Some good qualities for you to have are adventurousness, resourcefulness, energy, helpfulness, and a sense of humor.

If you have lots of outdoor skills and dread being cooped up inside an office, then you should read *Careers for Nature Lovers and Other Outdoor Types,* by Louise Miller (VGM Career Horizons, 4255 West Touhy Avenue, Lincolnwood, IL 60646-1975). Maybe you should consider being a plant farmer or a park ranger.

8. Considering moving? Don't just play spin-the-globe. Every year, *Money* magazine ranks the best places in America to live. Such books as *Places Rated Almanac: Your Guide to Finding the Best Places to Live in America,* by Richard Boyer and David Savageau, are constantly being updated to keep up with the changing landscape. These guides compare metropolitan areas in categories including job outlook, crime, health, transportation, education, the arts, recreation, and climate. Most books include the percentage of increase in new jobs along with job projections for the next five years. A simple enough task, researching the area where you are going to attend school, work, or open a business might give you some new insights or save you from a big mistake.

9. Almost any ability can contribute to your career. If you can do something for yourself, maybe you can do it for others. Hobby shops, hardware stores, libraries, and bookstores all have manuals on building bookshelves, cabinets, and other kinds of furniture, putting up wall coverings, designing curtains and shades, installing windows and skylights, and so on. Home and auto repair, gardening, and cooking are always in demand.

In almost every area lies a business opportunity. Ideally, you should combine your natural capabilities with popular growth fields. If you're twenty years old and can't seem to box up your toys yet, and would rather watch a Slinky go down the stairs or set up your Play-Doh macaroni factory than go to a rock concert, maybe you should be working in toy sales, manufacture, or design. If you have accumulated enough speeding tickets to pass your college years in jail should they go unpaid, and haven't had any accidents, then maybe you should consider being an ambulance driver.

I'm not joking.

By the age of twelve I could be found at the horseracing track more often than in school. It was rewarding: I taught myself handicapping, and so I often won. An interest in games and gambling addicted me to poker, blackjack, backgammon, gin, and chess, and led me to learn about probability. This interest later helped me when I was trading options on the floor of the stock exchange—a career built on an interest in games.

Some Common Occupational Pitfalls

First of all, don't have unrealistic aims for your educational experience. School will not teach you what to do with your life. Don't operate under the misconception that it is supposed to provide any function other than baby-sitting and providing you with basic education and socialization skills. Determining your interests does not happen automatically and may have little to do with the subjects taught in school. You've got to make it a point to find out for yourself, and to start as early as possible.

If you haven't yet decided the direction your career will take, and are working toward doing so, that's fine. However, if you're waiting for school or divine intervention to solve the problem, it's time to be proactive.

Don't, however, rely on someone else—for example, someone who has promised you a job. There's no guarantee that it will work out well for the both of you, or that the job will be waiting when you're finally ready.

Choose your career for the right reasons. Avoid pressures from family and friends who think they know what you should do. Advice can be nice, but you don't want to be in a position where you're living out someone else's dreams or trying to fulfill others' needs, even if they are paying for college. It can be hard to separate your needs and values from those of your parents, since the latter were probably an integral part of your education. But you must.

On the danger list are mothers who want their sons to be doctors; fathers who want their daughters to be housewives or super-career women; and parents who assume their children will work in family businesses. Parents often see their children as extensions of themselves to the point where they think you should both agree on the details of your education and career. Families are useful, however, in that parents and other relatives *can* give you valuable insights into different jobs they have had, help you to network, or even allow you to observe the office or plant where they work.

View guidance counselors, too, with caution. Many are accustomed to advising students to train for jobs based on salaries and benefits rather than on what career will provide intellectual stimulation and emotional satisfaction to the individual. Also, counselors tend to judge your aptitudes strictly by grades and test results and not according to your personal preferences.

Make sure you don't base your goals on a hunger for prestige. A high-profile job with lots of perks and a flashy company car doesn't guarantee a satisfying day on the job, especially if the position isn't challenging or stimulating.

Beware of aptitude tests. Unfortunately, choosing a career is not just a matter of answering questions about yourself and plugging it all into a formula. Supposedly, such tests allow you to realize things about yourself, such as whether you work better independently or as part of a team. You should already know these things about yourself. After all, you've been able to observe your own actions and attitudes for years. It's ridiculous to assume that you should be a forest ranger because you don't like to deal with aggravating customers, or that you should clean cages at the zoo because you love your pet cat.

This is a diverse list of don'ts, but the theme remains the same: If you're doing something for *any* other reason than that it interests you, you probably won't be very good at it in the long run. Sure, you may be proficient at a given job, and better at it than lots of other folks, but if it doesn't spark a passion in you, then you are not going to be a career entrepreneur or an innovator in your field.

Don't forget to consider the things you dislike. Learn from everything including former jobs, chores around the house, and unpleasant schoolwork. Aside from doing dishes and taking out the garbage, there are a lot of tasks some people don't mind, and actually enjoy doing, while others find them pure torture. Gardening, shopping, traveling, public speaking, and reading are all examples of common activities; some people are dedicated to them, some are ambivalent about them, and others are absolutely terrified of them.

At the age of sixteen I made a list of summer employment and odd jobs I had worked at: lemonade-stand operator, newspaper route carrier, magician for children's parties, apple cider presser, driveway snow shoveler, file clerk, car-wash attendant, business-card printer, camp counselor, short-order cook, research assistant, and bakery manager. (In this last instance I was the only employee, and thus referred to myself as the manager.) Except for my brief stint as a magician, I can't explain how much I hated those jobs. When I think back to *any* of them, I shudder. Highlights: delivering papers at 5:30 A.M. in Buffalo through four feet of snow; being bitten by a miniature schnauzer; working as a camp counselor while being allergic to everything outside including grass, sun, and the five-year-olds; finding out the restaurant where I cooked had been supplied with kangaroo meat for two months. (Not only was I serving it, but I had consumed enough myself to start measuring the length of my strides for any visible increases that could be considered leaps.) Restauranting *can* be very lucrative, but you'll never see *me* running (ruining) Le Cirque.

Suffering does not have to be a part of working.

Pinpoint weaknesses and avoid them. A few of the most common are an inability to deal with customers, shyness, lack of organization, and failure to meet deadlines. If the career or area of study you choose involves constantly fighting a weakness, it's not going to be very enjoyable. This does not mean you should avoid challenges or that you can't overcome weaknesses. If, however, your mathematical skills are weak and you find the subject tedious, then why pursue a career such as accounting, which involves a lot of computation?

Think about your strengths in the same way. Common examples are an ability to pay attention to details, or a specific skill such as mastery of a language.

Let's say you're a bit compulsive about paying bills on time, returning phone calls, and turning off all the lights. Friends might find this aggravating, but these habits would be greatly appreciated in an office, laboratory, or research postion. You're trying to work everything possible about yourself into this career. Not everything is going to fit, but at least try to be aware of your limitations and capabilities.

Along the same lines, ask yourself in which type of situations you feel most comfortable. Do you enjoy large groups of people, such as you would find at an enormous bank, or do you prefer the privacy of a small office that only deals with customers over the phone? Do you like to be indoors or outside? Would the noise of a large factory or commodities exchange bother you? Is a library or school too quiet? Do you have any phobias? Some people are terrified by hospitals and could never consider doing any type of job in such an environment. Do you prefer working with older people, younger people, or those who are the same age as yourself? Does it matter? Do you like directing others or being directed? Believe it or not, not everybody wants to be in charge. Do you want a job where there is constant change, such as in advertising, journalism, or political campaigns? Or do you prefer something with lots of consistency, such as repairing appliances or being a pharmacist or a dentist?

How dedicated are you to your hobbies? If it's popular, such as flying kites, collecting coins, building birdhouses, or setting up ant farms, it has potential. Obviously, if you bought supplies for your hobby—such as books, kits, magazines, food for your tropical fish—then somebody sold it you. If you were able to buy these things, then obviously there are other enthusiasts who are interested in reading literature, adding to their collections, browsing in a store dedicated to the hobby, or attending a conference or show about it. What is it about your hobby that brings out the best in you?

You don't necessarily *have* to open a corner store for tracing genealogy, start a magazine for taffy makers, or sell model airplane kits. I'm just pointing out that a market exists. (On the other hand, if your big thing is gluing Coke bottle caps together, making gum-wrapper chains, or collecting beach glass, there is not much of a market unless you call yourself an artist. And that's a totally different thing from building a hobby into a business.) If you do make your hobby into a business, that's great, because you will definitely enjoy it, though there's no guarantee that it will be profitable. What you can definitely gain through your hobbies is a knowledge of where your passions lie.

Back to having an ant farm: If you love collecting bugs, maybe you should study insects or agriculture in school, or work in a related field. If you love white-water rafting, maybe you can become an Outward Bound instructor or study physical education in school. Hobbies you've enjoyed for many years can often be the starting point for identifying the activities that really motivate and excite you.

In this process of discovery, you're going to have to be active and grow. Seeking is not a spectator sport.

Encouraging Change

Let's face it, people do grow and change. In fact, they *need* to change. If they didn't, 50 percent of marriages wouldn't end in divorce, and people wouldn't color their hair or switch religions.

The Chinese written word for *crisis* combines the characters for *danger* and *opportunity*. Don't avoid changing your circumstances and risk limiting your exposure to the world. Instead, actively pursue it! For example, try to spend some time in another country, whether it's a high school exchange program, a college semester abroad, or a work-related project. Don't feel that because you can't afford to travel, the only other options are getting a backpack, a Eurail Pass, and a guide to bed-and-breakfasts, or becoming a flight attendant. Peterson's Guides has a number of books about combining work with travel including the following: *Teaching English Abroad; Directory of Overseas Summer Jobs; Work Your Way Around the World;* and several others. Each guide contains sources and advice including where to find recruitment agencies and how to prepare for a job and overcome red tape.

View any change in school, location, work, or

other aspect of your lifestyle as a positive experience filled with hidden opportunites.

On a small scale, participate in different activities at school or in the community, so that you come into contact with new people. Request the opportunity to try working in different areas of your job.

Continue to take adult education classes if you're out of school, even if it's just for fun or to explore a hobby; you may discover that you have an aptitude for something, or that there is a business angle.

It may take ten years to find your niche, but you have to draw on all available resources and start experimenting.

Developing a Personal Style

Accept responsibility, especially if you have gone through life shunning leadership because of the extra time and work it takes. This is a way to learn valuable management and organizational skills. Whether it's in a church or school organization, a local committee, a political campaign, or your own special-interest group, sign up as treasurer, secretary, or president. You'll be surprised by how many people appreciate your work (and how many don't), and the contacts you will make.

Help others. Broaden your perspective by being aware of other people's special needs. Tutor the underprivileged, volunteer at a halfway house, provide transportation to the elderly, or just help a neighbor paint his or her walls.

Luck is synonymous with recognizing opportunities. *Make* your own luck by continuously seeking information and thus preparing to seize each opportunity that presents itself.

6

Do for Pay
What You Would Do for Play

Doing What Comes Naturally
Sugar Ray Leonard, the prizefighter, told a group of
students at Harvard, "I consider myself blessed. I
consider you blessed. We've all been blessed with
God-given talents. Mine just happens to be beatin'
people up." After winning a 1976 Olympic gold
medal, Leonard was not showered with offers of commercial endorsements. So he put his gloves back on
and had one loss in thirty-three fights over a two-
and-a-half-year period. He made over $35 million,
and endorsements, speaking engagements, and offers
to appear as a commentator on televised boxing
matches soon followed.

Maybe your talent is giving back-rubs. Or maybe
it's teaching kids, sewing, writing music, training sea
lions, or sportscasting. The point is, if you do what
you love, you'll probably be good at it, and "the
money will follow," as the saying goes. When you
are doing something you enjoy, it no longer seems
like work. Playing a basketball game takes a lot of
concentration and energy, but it doesn't seem like
work to the players.

Take a look at some entrepreneurs who parlayed
their working situations and experience into suc-

cessful large- or small-scale ventures. What these people have in common is that after taking time to learn about many different things that attracted their interest, they pursued and built on something they really understood.

Keep in mind that even more important, although probably less spectacular, are the people who can't be recognized quite as easily. For instance, the people who catered the last wedding you attended, or installed the floor in your kitchen. They probably started out several years ago working on a shoestring budget, with maybe one other person, driving around in the family station wagon trying to get jobs.

• Larry Harmon was studying to be a gynecologist when he gave it up to become a clown, calling himself Bozo. Public and private engagements eventually led to a popular children's television show. Harmon took his success a step further by founding Bozo College, which currently has satellites all around the world teaching Bozology. After passing courses in juggling, production, makeup and other clown essentials, you can get your red nose and have guaranteed job placement. Mr. Harmon recently commented that he is anxiously watching for the first female Bozo graduate.

• William Gates learned to program a computer in the seventh grade, and by the time he was seventeen he was adapting the computer language BASIC in order to create an operating system for the first microcomputer. He went on to design PCs and software packages. Gates has been CEO of Microsoft for the past ten years. He owns 35 percent of the company's stock, worth over 6 billion dollars.

• In 1992, Nell Caitlin Parker started her successful garment-bag manufacturing business, En

Fleur, in under three weeks with only a few thousand dollars. After ten years as a fashion photographer, she noticed that businesswomen didn't have any non-leather garment bags that would conveniently carry one or two dresses and suits. She designed her bags out of attractive tapestries with earthy Southwestern themes, including pockets for shoes and cosmetics, and brought them to a fashion accessories trade show at the Javits Center in New York. After three days, Parker wrote $100,000 in orders (as well as selling individual sets to a large number of admiring buyers), and expanded her line to include knapsacks, tote bags, pillows, tapestry-covered photo albums, and sachets.

• Greg Smith, a morticians' school dropout, started Grave Line Tours, a very successful company that provides only one activity: a Hollywood tour of locations where celebrities have died, complete with factual commentary describing the incidents. At thirty dollars, the tour is one of the most expensive in Hollywood as well as one of the most popular.

• Ten years ago, Lu Clinton started baking Sugar Spoon Cheesecakes in her North Platte, Nebraska, home to earn extra income to help put three of her four children through college. After watching a segment of the *Today* show, which featured the wife of a U.S. Senator who was operating a gourmet bakery in Boston, Mrs. Clinton ordered six springform pans and studied the pages of *Bon Appetit* magazine for recipes. Mrs. Clinton would load her Subaru with cheesecake-filled coolers every day and deliver orders to surrounding towns. These days, six different food distributors deliver her cheesecakes to forty-nine states (all except Hawaii) and Canada. She is negotiating for distributorships in Australia and Hawaii,

and is investigating an opportunity to do business in
Japan.

• Henry Yuen and Daniel Kwoh were salaried
researchers for TRW until their company, Gemstar,
made $40 million in 1991. The inventors developed
VCR Plus, a system for punching a series of numbers
into a VCR that directs it to tape a particular program. The numbers are carried in television guides
and newpapers next to listings. The two are currently
taking this success a step further with another company, iPlus Incorporated, which puts out a similar
system that advertisers can use to deliver specific
information to interested consumers. Instead of following up an ad by calling an 800 number for more
information, the consumer simply punches in the
listed VCR code, to be regaled with a more in-depth
commercial.

• Ed Chavez was a marketing manager for Fri-
gidaire when he saw his opportunity on a trip to
Japan: No one had a garbage disposal and didn't
know they needed one. In 1985, Chavez launched his
company, Anaheim Marketing, with a credit card.
Now he's president, and the firm is worth $5 million,
with no end in sight. His company sells garbage dis-
posals in Europe as well as the Far East.

Navigating Your Route

The average individual is probably going to work
ten thousand days at one of the millions of different
types of available jobs or, more likely, at some combination of jobs. In addition, two to three million
brand-new jobs are being added to the marketplace
each year (over forty thousand per week). In total,
you'll probably spend over one-third of your life
working. How many jobs are you aware of? Search-

ing for an occupation is not about knowing things, it's about knowing where to find things.

If you love movies, for example, you don't necessarily have to be an actor or a producer. *The TV and Movie Business*, by Harvey Rachlin, lists over one hundred different jobs in this industry. Just a few: electronic editor, model builder, graphic designer, boom operator, and story analyst. *Ross Reports Television: Casting, Scripts, Production* is published monthly for actors, writers, technicians, and other TV personnel, and lists names and addresses for everything from advertising and talent agencies to variety shows ("Saturday Night Live," "Late Night with David Letterman") and program packagers. *Variety, Back Stage, Actors Resource,* and *The Hollywood Reporter,* available at the magazine rack or by subscription, contain listings of auditions, positions available, classes offered, and industry news.

The problem with deciding upon your dream job is that you can't be sure what it's really like until you try it. So be prepared to make a number of attempts. If you've dreamed of being a stage manager all your life and finally achieve that goal, be prepared to find out that you may have had unrealistic expectations of what it would be like. At this point, a lot of people would nonetheless remain in the position. After all, it's what they *thought* they wanted. They end up feeling miserable, disappointed, and eventually trapped.

Also be prepared to accept that you may not have the aptitude for the particular job which you sincerely seek. If you somehow manage to get the job, it surely has to be a series of disappointments when you realize that you can't advance at a rate equivalent to more skilled co-workers, make sufficient contributions to the company, or have a sense of personal fulfillment. That's why it's so important to examine the talents and abilities you *know* that you possess, and to be realistic about your physical or intellectual limitations.

The most difficult thing can be to have a lot of potential or many aptitudes. For example, what if you are an outstanding science and math student and receive scholarships to expensive schools, but would rather become a craftsman and make stained glass? You'll be the recipient of a considerable amount of advice, criticism, and lectures about how "you're ruining your life and you don't even know it." Now, if making stained glass was your *only* talent and you couldn't even read, the same people would be relieved that you're happy to pursue life as an artisan. The problem with the American Dream is that most people translate the success that it embodies directly into earning potential. But just because you have the ability to be a nuclear physicist doesn't mean you're wasting your life or cheating mankind by becoming a tree surgeon.

Realize that different careers are meaningful to different types of people. For example, teaching can be either very fulfilling or extremely frustrating, depending on your feelings about your purpose in life, what you expect to contribute to society, and whether you have a rapport with children. Some people think that the only way to truly contribute and make the world better is actively to change it, and thus they go into politics. Others are disgusted by political life. A stockbroker may feel that he is contributing to the economy of the country by bringing buyers and sellers together, while a social worker may think the broker isn't doing anything valuable. The right job results in high self-esteem for the person performing it. Every career can be held up to outside criticism.

Devotion and commitment are necessary to the pursuit of an enriching life. Whatever you are trying to accomplish, it will probably not pay very well at the beginning. As you learn and develop skills, however, your income will improve. In the meantime, though, it might be necessary to make sacrifices such as working two jobs, performing boring, tedious labor just to pay the bills, or going through school or training programs you don't enjoy, but that are ultimately necessary.

My first job on the floor of the stock exchange, for example, paid $150 a week, which is less than an unemployment check. Almost *all* of my money went into rent. This resulted in my not having heat in my apartment, using a plastic beach chair for a sofa, an excercise mat on the floor for a bed, and the windowsill as a refrigerator in the winter, just to save the thirteen dollars a month it cost for the electricity to run the fridge. I knew that everyone had to start somewhere, and hoped that the situation wouldn't last forever. The sacrifice was definitely worth it. After a year I was able to afford a better apartment (with heat), and eventually I achieved a very nice lifestyle.

People magazine highlights individuals involved with some major event, artistic accomplishment, or business achievement. It's easy to infer from profiles in magazines that a person has been on the right track all along and never doubted that success would prevail (particularly if it's a full-blown rags-to-riches story). Rather than a quick account of someone's ascent to fame, miraculous triumph over adversity, or film debut, it's much more realistic to read booklength biographies or autobiographies of politicians, athletes, entertainers, or anybody who has experienced interesting challenges in his or her life. Full biographies give a truer sense of the ups and downs, gains and setbacks in accomplishing a goal.

For example, when you view Joan Rivers as an

Emmy Award–winning talk show host, it looks as if she's been successful since the day she stepped on a stage. In reality, her long, difficult road to stardom is surprising and tremendously inspirational, as I found out when I read her autobiography, *Enter Talking*. After college, she defied her parents and led the starving-artist life of a Greenwich Village comic and writer. Professionals counseled her to quit. Finally, at the age of fifty, she became Johnny Carson's permanent guest host. Rivers left to start her own show, which was subsequently canceled. She has written books, spent forty weeks on the road some years, and starred on Broadway. Through sheer drive and determination, she persisted despite failures and disappointments until she finally beat the odds. Before learning this information, I assumed that she had always accomplished whatever she set out to do with ease. Joan Rivers is the living embodiment of the message, Get up, get out, fail, try again—over and over and over.

Try it. Look in a recent edition of *Who's Who in America: Geographical/Professional Area Index*. Even if you're not interested in other people and have never watched a talk show in your life, this exercise still has networking potential. It's possible to find people in your area who might be worth contacting. This is not to say that Michelle Pfeiffer is going to return your call in order to chat about the movie biz, but other professionals will often respond to a sincere letter asking for an introduction, answers to specific questions, or career advice.

Other people's stories may not be able to save you from making mistakes, but they can certainly help you pick yourself up and get started again. Anyone interested in politics, history, or world affairs should read about the fascinating and tumultuous career of Winston Churchill. When invited to address the graduating class at Oxford University in his later years, he walked to the lectern and said, "Never, never, never give up," and returned to his seat.

Remember—any of these people could have stayed put, but instead they "did what comes naturally" to succeed "their way."

7

Homing in on Specific Fields

Is it possible to find a career that thrills you as much as leading exercise classes intoxicates Richard Simmons?

Well, finding meaningful work is a path that changes every time you make a choice or a decision. We are all familiar with meeting someone who changes our lives—a teacher, a roommate, or a spouse—and we've all had experiences that have done this in large and small ways: for example, being involved in a school activity, having a car accident, helping a friend through a difficult time. *All* the things that happen to you on a daily basis should keep shaping and refining your plans and desires.

If you're completely undecided about what path to take, forget about setting long-term goals for the time being. Instead, the trick is to get involved in a number of different areas in order to try them out. Too many self-help gurus preach visualization, self-actualization, and trips to the Himalayas. You need an idea of what you want to do and what direction you will take, but picturing in your mind exactly what it is and how your life will be when you achieve it is about as useful as sitting around wondering if you really did learn everything you need to know in kindergarten. How can you possibly fashion any sort of plan when you don't even have your interests or op-portunities sorted out? If you feel pressured to set specific goals, it's because there are too many time-management, lifestyle-efficiency people on the loose giving seminars on setting goals for eating, breathing and sleeping, while prioritizing your daily bathroom routine.

I'm not telling you not to have *any* goals, or just to "go with the flow" because "whatever happens, happens." Far from it; it's just that a goal comes *after,* not before, you get your bearings.

Where the Jobs Are

Do some homework and use common sense. Look around you. Heighten your awareness of career pos-sibilities. Start with your own neighborhood, town, or city. What types of businesses is the area known for? *City and State Directories in Print* is in most libraries and lists thousands of local, city, and state publica-tions not found in national and international direc-tories. Also, every state has at least one federal employment job information center that can assist you in learning about available jobs and their require-ments, and procedures for applying. Check under Department of Labor in the government offices sec-tion of your phonebook.

At one time, my hometown of Buffalo, New York, was a blue-collar steel town. Now it's a thriving professional center with lots of clothing and food re-tailers profiting from Canadian money being spent just over the border. In San Francisco, it's obvious that tourism is the hottest game in town. Those tour-ists can't get enough of the cable cars and sea lions, while downtown, Bank of America is the major em-ployer of local financiers. Specialty shops for bikes and biking accessories are another popular item, despite the city's hills. New Jersey is becoming for biotechnology what Texas once was for oil. Almost every area has some type of industry for which it's known, and a list of companies operating locally. In the October 19, 1992, issue, *Business Week* listed the following locations as "America's new growth regions." (Note: The cities, listed alphabetically by state, indicate the center of a larger surrounding region.)

Tucson, Arizona
Major industries: Lasers, electro-optics
40 companies, 1,000 jobs
Start-ups: Wyko, Photometrics

San Diego, California
Major industries: Biotechnology, communications
163 companies, 11,000 jobs
Start-ups: Hybritech, Qualcomm

Washington, D.C.
Major industry: Systems integration
1,100 companies, 80,000 jobs
Start-ups: Legent, Landmark Systems

Orlando, Florida
Major industries: Systems integration
1,100 companies, 80,000
Start-ups: Legent, Landmark Systems

Boise, Idaho
Major industries: Semiconductor chips, laser printers
25 companies, 14,300 jobs
Start-ups: Micron Technology, Extended Systems

Champaign/Urbana, Illinois
Major industry: Software

63 companies, 3,500 jobs
Start-ups: Wolfram Research, Kuck & Associates

Minneapolis/St. Paul, Minnesota
Major industries: Medical instruments, health care
500 companies, 40,000 jobs
Start-ups: ATS Medical, Pharmacia Deltec

Princeton, New Jersey
Major industries: Biotechnology,
telecommunications
400 companies, 132,400 jobs
Start-ups: Cytogen, Liposome

Corning, New York
Major industries: Ceramics, electronics packaging
110 companies, 31,500 jobs
Start-ups: Hi-Tech Ceramics, Xylon Materials

Philadelphia, Pennsylvania
Major industries: Biotechnology, medical products
500 companies, 166,000 jobs
Start-ups: Magainin, Cephalon

Austin, Texas
Major industries: Computer manufacturing, chips
450 companies, 55,000 jobs
Start-ups: Dell Computer, CompuAdd

Richardson, Texas
Major industries: Telecommunications systems and
components, software
500 companies, 50,000 jobs
Start-ups: Intervoice, Cyrix, Convex Computer

Provo/Orem, Utah
Major industry: Software

175 companies, 12,000 jobs
Start-ups: WordPerfect, Novell

Salt Lake City, Utah
Major industries: Medical devices, artificial organs
75 companies, 8,000 jobs
Start-ups: Becton-Dickinson Vascular Access, Utah
Medical

In addition to scoping out your own backyard, check on areas in which you would like to live or attend school (possible internships), and make notes when you go on vacation. (Just think, perhaps you can live and work year-round where you water ski each summer!)

Consult *Dun's Business Rankings* or *Moody's Industrial Manual,* both of which rate companies. What are the largest companies in your town or city, and what do they do? What type of start-ups (new companies or businesses) have begun in the past few years? Larger plants and factories may even offer tours. Call the chamber of commerce for local business listings, and then call the companies and ask if they have some type of arrangement. You may even wind up with a person from public relations to give you a private information session.

Most of us see several large buildings where a hundred or so people race in every morning before nine and fall back out around five in the afternoon. What goes on in there? Who owns it? What do they make or do? The U.S. Labor Department's Bureau of Labor Statistics has prepared a *Career Guide to Industries* to tackle specific questions about different industries—for example, jobs that can be entered from high school, jobs that do not require specialized education or training, opportunities for acquiring skills, and earnings of key occupations and prospects for upward mobility in them.

Most estimates tell you that anywhere from 50 to 80 percent of jobs are found through networking. Not only are most jobs found this way, but so is the information about them. The first line of attack is to go through your relationships: family, friends, acquaintances, fellow workers, boss, teachers, doctor, dentist, lawyer, minister/rabbi, and any other personal or professional relationships.

High school or college placement offices may be able to provide names of graduates already working in areas in which you are interested. Call them and ask for a tour of the workplace or information about their job. A recent graduate, probably on the bottom rung of the company, is able to give you a much different view from that of an executive or a veteran employee. Just be careful not to take up too much of the person's time. Have a list of short questions ready, such as the following:

- What do you like about the job?

- What parts of your education have helped?

- Do you think this business has a good future?

- What does it pay at different levels?

- If it's a public company, how is the stock doing?

Most people are more than willing to give you five or ten minutes if you're a friend of a friend or even if you're cold-calling. Just don't pester the person for information or recommendations so they're unwilling to help the next person that comes along. Always send a thank-you note. If you are seeking a job, it is not inappropriate to enclose a copy of your resumé at that time.

These types of short conversations are the best way to find out the real version of what a job is like. You might find out about company politics, "corporate culture," the financial outlook (is the company a sinking ship or has it just announced a major dividend?), and even what the cafeteria's food is like. A person from the company marketing department, personnel office, or campus recruiter is not in the business of telling you anything but the most flattering facts (and distortions) about the company and position, just as the annual report is designed to present things in the best possible light. Also, your in-house contact is more likely to give you names of competitors or other employees whom you might then contact.

The next step in networking is to contact trade organizations. All professions have at least one organization. The *Encyclopedia of Associations* is published annually, and should be in the library or any career center. It's a guide to more than 22,000 national and international organizations, including environmental and agricultural, governmental, technological, natural and social science, cultural, health and medical, public affairs, foreign interest, ethnic, religious, hobby, and athletic and sports. It contains listings of labor unions, associations, federations, chambers of commerce, and fan clubs. The *Encyclopedia of Associations: Regional, State and Local Organizations* contains more than 47,000 entries arranged by state and city, and includes local chapters of national groups. Find out about meetings, conventions, bulletins, and types of career networking provided. See if you can get names of people to contact, maybe even in your area. Also, see if you can locate any retirees to ask for help.

They may have a bit more time and the patience to help someone.

Some professional organizations, such as those for teachers, entrepreneurs, and public speakers, have student chapters. They offer activities, scholarships, and ways to learn more about the trade. To find these, you have to work backwards by finding your interest area in the *Encyclopedia of Associations*, or some similar type of guide, and calling to inquire.

A great source to find what types of careers are available (but often overlooked because it's so obvious) is your local Yellow Pages. As NYNEX claims, "If it's out there, it's in here." Read the Yellow Pages as you would a magazine, and if something sounds interesting or unfamiliar, make a call and inquire about the business. Ask for names of people in the field, and inquire about trade publications and business associations. Talk to these people and read any materials you can come up with. They'll contain the next set of clues in your search.

When I was seventeen and decided to become a stockbroker, I called six brokers listed in the Yellow Pages. It must have been a slow day, because someone took the time to talk with me at every office, even though I wasn't opening an account. Knowing nothing about the job, here's what I learned in fifteen minutes for the cost of six local phone calls:

• You don't need a college degree.

• Some brokers work on salary and commission and some just on commission.

• If you're a good salesperson and know what you're doing, you can make unlimited money.

• You have to take a registered representative exam.

• A company has to sponsor you.

• You have to be twenty-one to take the exam.

Obviously, it was the last bit of information that temporarily killed the project for me. The next two calls were long distance. First I had to call information to get the number for the American Stock Exchange in New York City. In five minutes I found out the following:

• They accepted applications for entry-level work.

• A high school diploma was necessary.

• One had to be sixteen years old to apply and only eighteen years old to trade stocks.

I packed up and moved to New York the following week. (But you certainly don't have to be that impetuous.)

Don't feel shy or stupid about calling and asking for information. The person on the other end doesn't know who you are. The worst thing that can happen is that he or she will hang up or transfer your call.

Keep a file. Every chamber of commerce will send you information about the area and the types of businesses that can be found there—complete with names, addresses, and phone numbers. They'll tell you about population, the major industries and crops, tourist attractions, and cultural organizations, and probably enclose a coupon from the local homemade fudge shop. Use these resources; your tax dollars are paying for them.

Keep trade magazines, industry newsletters, and specific articles you find interesting. Trade magazines and industry newsletters are filled with advertising that can give you ideas or help in obtaining more information. Here are two examples: A magazine called *Snack Food* has information on upcoming exhibitions, suppliers, packaging, "snack wars," and a no-postage-necessary card to send for information on manufacturers, processors, distributors, wholesalers, food brokers, and more. A newspaper called *Footwear News,* published weekly by the Fairchild Fashion and Merchandising Group, contains information about new products, an update on the latest styles in the big cities, a study comparing shoe manufacture in Taiwan and the United States, and a trade show calendar. The last few pages of trade periodicals usually contain listings of services related to the business, complete with a help-wanted section.

Also, hang on to flyers of any small businesses or services that catch your interest, along with the names and numbers of any people who may be potential future contacts.

All public companies (ones that are listed on a stock exchange) will send you free copies of their annual reports and any other available information if you call and request it. They actually want to encourage your interest, because you represent a potential stockholder. In examining the annual report, don't worry about the financial parts. Instead, read about what businesses the company is involved in, if they're expanding or cutting back, whom they sell to, and where the headquarters and plants are located.

Once you've explored various industries, look at types of positions in these fields.

Selecting an Occupation
Think about the future of an existing career. Technological change and the shift in the country's economy can account for periods of growth and de-

cline in the demand for skilled workers. Use the *Occupational Outlook Quarterly,* annual reports, changing school curricula, and any other observations as a guide to determining where the jobs in your field of choice will be in the future. Remember, the U.S. economy is projected to provide 24 million more jobs in 2005 than it did in 1990, an increase of 20 percent.* Occupations expected to decline in the period include electrical and electronic assemblers, electronic semiconductor processors, railroad conductors and yardmasters, stenographers, farmers, and industrial truck and tractor operators.

The following are some examples of jobs likely to be hot and growing in the near future:

• *High Tech.* Computer maintenance, computer software, robotics, artificial intelligence, computer graphics, data-bank management. New products and state-of-the-art equipment are revolutionizing all fields of medicine, dentistry, physical therapy, life extension, and even cosmetics. All the new patents and licensing will also call for more attorneys.

• *General Maintenance.* Cleaning, fixing, painting, installing, and plumbing, as an increasing number of apartment houses, stores, schools, hospitals, and hotels are built.

• *Health Care.* Nursing, physical therapy, elder care, child care, medical and lab technicians, and home health care. Preventive medicine will call for more counselors, diet coaches, and nutrition therapists.

---

*Jay M. Berman and Theresa A. Cosca, "The Job Outlook in Brief, 1990–2005," *Occupational Outlook Quarterly,* Spring 1992.

• *Environmentally Related Jobs.* Chemical waste removal and treatment, community waste disposal, recycling, environmental law. More scientists and consultants will be needed in all these areas.

• *Stress Reduction.* Therapists and counselors of all kinds. Travel and spas dedicated to alleviating stress. Also look for an increase in demand for podiatrists as people are advised to take up more exercise.

• *Security and Security Systems.* Locks, alarms, floodlights, fences, and guards to serve an increasingly crowded and crime-ridden society.

• *Education.* Adult illiteracy is a national crisis, and it is anticipated that 65 percent of all U.S. corporations will have remedial education programs for employees by the year 2000. Also, the demand for kindergarten and primary-grade teachers should increase as the large number of teachers now in their forties and fifties reach retirement age.

• *Food Preparation and Home Economics.* Chefs, food preparers, and shoppers to assist the increasing number of working mothers.

• *Marketing and Promotion.* Promotion has become ubiquitous, with ads on grocery carts, billboards, and bus shelters. Everything you need and don't need (but want anyway) is becoming available through phone, fax, television, and video ordering. Additionally, increasing foreign competition requires more public relations.

• *Appliance and Auto Repair.* As occupations and education become increasingly specialized, fewer people can make even simple repairs or perform basic maintenance on such things as lawn mowers, computers, appliances, and plumbing. The Maytag repairman, contrary to myth, is not a lonely guy.

• *Telecommunications.* Cable TV and cellular communications will certainly expand. Sure, everyone in L.A. has a cellular phone and is now busy installing a car fax, but even farmers are entering the market by using cellular phones to order parts for machinery and exchange time-sensitive information. U.S. companies are pursuing the international telecommunications business by acquiring licenses or merging with companies that have them. Many countries, such as Thailand, mainland China, and Taiwan, currently have only about one telephone for every fifty people. Telephone service is so inefficient in some parts of Mexico that to call across town, people send the call to the United States and have it transferred back down.

• *Truck Transportation.* As more large corporations offer direct distribution, and as warehousing declines, more truckers make more trips. Consumers are obsessed with freshness and quick delivery. Companies rely heavily on truckers to service this need.

• *Entertainment.* The United States continues to dominate the global marketplace in films, game shows, and music videos. There are opportunities for technicians, writers, animators, and musicians, among others.

• *Hospitality.* Hotels, shopping, and restaurants serve a mobile society with a high rate of tourism and a demand for a quality lifestyle.

• *Financial Services.* Don't let the savings-and-loan crisis or periodic slumps in real estate discourage you from pursuing a career in banking or finance. Americans are investors and consumers. We purchase stocks and bonds, own real estate, acquire collectibles, buy franchises, and invest in savings programs. The strength of our economy is in large measure the product of our combined investments. Every town and city where income is rising will require more banking, stock brokerage, mortgage companies, financial planning, accounting, and tax preparation. Perhaps more so than anyone else in the world, we enjoy an ever-expanding variety of investments to choose from, along with the freedom to decide where our money should go. According to the May 2, 1992, edition of *The Economist,* one in four American families owns shares in a mutual fund. Funds have net assets of more than $1.4 trillion (up from $240 billion a decade ago), and these may top $3.5 trillion by 2000.

European countries and Japan are even trying to emulate our full-service financial shopping centers. Banks and brokerage firms are quickly setting up operations overseas and are eager to train people with business backgrounds to run them. These innovations represent only the tip of the economic iceberg.

Of course, you don't *have* to do anything mainstream; there are more jobs you never heard of that can be fascinating and rewarding. You can be a pyrotechnist, brewmaster, perfumer, Antarctic crew member, racetrack announcer, weatherman, shepherd, lumberjack, wine steward, chocolatier, repo man, bomb disposal technician, or miniature-golf pro. It's true! As a miniature golf competitor, you can collect several thousand dollars in prizes, while the winner of the national tournament can pocket up to sixteen thousand dollars in prize money. There are forty openings for smoke-jumpers every year. These people parachute into wooded areas to mount first-strike containment efforts against shifts in large fires. They receive a salary of $18,300 and may have to parachute only fifteen times a year. For more unusual occupations, consult *Offbeat Careers: The Directory of Unusual Work*, by Al Sacharov. Here are some suggestions directly from the Yellow Pages: model-car racer, mothproofer, salt miner, orchid grower, snow maker, tortilla and tamale maker, water taxi operator, furniture stripper, and piano tuner.

The information you need to start researching your career, and possibly find your dream job, is just a phone call away—and if you decide to use the Yellow Pages, the number is already listed right there!

8

Starting on Your Way

Now that you have an impression of your ideal field, best opportunities, and most promising job area, how do you get there?

Getting the Inside Scoop

It's time to really start hoarding information before committing any money or work hours. Talk to friends, friends' parents, your sisters and brothers, relatives, and people at your church or synagogue. Think of everyone you know, and make sure you know exactly what their jobs are. Ask people what *other* jobs they have had. You may be surprised to find out that your sixty-five-year-old neighbor who spends the entire day in his garden was a colonel in the Korean War, or that your friend's mother ran a life insurance agency for ten years. Get the scoop. More often than not, these people would love to spend some time sharing their work experiences with you.

Let's say you want to be a makeup artist. If your friend's older brother works as an engineer at the local television station, ask who does the makeup there. Maybe you can stop in for a few minutes one day to watch and ask a few questions. Call the local modeling agencies and ask who does the makeup for photo shoots and fashion shows. Call the bridal shop and ask who does makeup for wedding parties.

If you want to be a nutritionist, ask your doctor if he can recommend someone you can contact. Stop at the local fitness center and see if they work with anyone. Go to the hospital and retirement center and see how a nutritionist works at these facilities. After all, once you graduate from school, you'll have to choose a working environment.

Talk to people who are in the profession you are planning to enter. Find out if they like the work; if they don't, ask why not. Ask the salary range, and if there's room for growth in the field.

What else should you ask? Here are a few starters:

- What type of training is necessary?

- What are the best places to go for training?

- In what parts of the country are the best opportunities in this field?

- If you were entering this field now, what would you do differently?

You'll be amazed at how many people just tell you straight out how their original expectations were not fulfilled—for example, a person who went into the sciences and is now expected to spend more time getting published than doing original research. Or a person who studied early childhood development and ends up in an administrative position pushing paper at a school, but never actually works with children.

Another important thing these questions can help you decide is in what area of a particular field you will specialize. The person you are speaking with probably became entrenched in one aspect of the job over the past five or ten years and isn't in a position to change lanes, but *is* current on what is happening, and can steer you into an area that is more challenging, profitable, or exciting, or has a better future.

If it's your goal to be a journalist, a magazine editor with ten years' experience can tell you, better than any book of statistics or college writing class, the best way to pursue your career, the important courses to take or major in, the necessary experience or travel you should try to get, and the rewards of the job. If you don't have a degree, find out if the experience you already have might be helpful. This may include military, home-care, travel, or volunteer work.

As for obtaining unusual jobs, the only way to get an idea of what it takes to enter them, when there are no schools or training programs to attend, is to find people who do them and, again, to pepper them politely with questions. Courses to be a repo man, beekeeper, band roadie, or fire-tower lookout are not likely to be listed in a course catalog. Subsequent openings probably won't be advertised in the local classified section or at employment agencies.

The best way to seek out the unusual jobs is by working backwards. In other words, you have to come up with the job, craft, or field, and then locate someone who does it. Most kids want to be firemen at one time or another because the job has high visibility, flashy red trucks, ladders, and news coverage. You probably first became aware of jobs you saw or with which you had direct contact, such as police officer, crossing guard, and teacher. It's the same way we become aware of any job — by watching someone else do it. Unusual occupation ideas can come from movies, television documentaries, books, and trips.

We are aware that most companies have the typical positions, such as salesperson, manager, marketer, information processor, and receptionist. But what about the product tester, the person who organizes conventions, the person whose job it is to find a writer and photographer for the annual report, the foreign currency trader (if the company does business overseas), and the travel coordinator?

Locate upcoming seminars, conventions, and professional groups' trade papers, newsletters and magazines. Also attend any relevant university lectures and chamber of commerce meetings. If you're a student, some expensive conventions may have a special student rate, or you might try to ask for one. You might even try asking for a press pass to write a story for your school or community newspaper. A person or organization running series of seminars or lectures will often allow you to attend one for free to see if you think the information will be of value to you. Attend trade shows. Check the local college or university library and bookstore for information on subjects related to the area you are researching.

If you're considering becoming a bona fide entrepreneur (running your own business, developing a major venture), find out what steps are typically involved in getting set up in that field so you can start preparing for it ahead of time, instead of squandering extra energy, organization, money, and time guessing the best procedures, or under- or overestimating the tasks at hand. If you're thinking of starting a pool-maintenance business, talk to your neighbors' pool cleaner. You'll find out about important detail work that's required before you can even begin: locating equipment and chemical suppliers, designing advertising, researching any legalities such as necessary forms, licenses, or tax statements. It adds up to lots of research, leg work, phone calls, and bookkeeping. Once you're aware of these aspects, it will help you decide whether you're willing to do what's involved in running a real pool business.

This principle of awareness also applies to larger-scale projects. Say you have a great plan for a ski resort and want to attract investors. You can't just walk in and explain your idea to a banker. You need a business plan, which includes financial projections, start-up costs, required investment, demographic studies to predict how well your business would succeed in a certain area, blueprints, licenses, and variances, among many other things. By finding people to talk to who have been involved in such ventures (for example, by speaking to the manager at the main lodge where you ski during winter vacations), you can learn from a pro how best to handle these tasks. You can also learn from their problems and mistakes, and perhaps they can refer you to good architects, lawyers, and so on. You might find the prospect so stimulating that you begin devoting all your energies to pursuing your goal—or so daunting you decide to scale down your idea. In either case, you'll at least be better prepared for the larger realities of starting the business you have in mind.

Real People

The experiences of real people who've succeeded in your fields of interest are especially valuable—in other words, celebrities, innovators, leaders, and other eminent citizens, living or dead. *Webster's New Biographical Dictionary* and *Who's Who in America* contain thousands of short sketches that are interesting and often entertaining. You may discover a new role model or find a new approach to your problems by studying how others went about accomplishing their goals.

If it's the President of the United States whose job you seek, read about the making of all the past presidents. Start with an encyclopedia, if you wish. You'll find out that a great percentage went to law school. If you want to be an actor, trace the careers of your favorite stars. You will probably discover that they had a lot of things in common, such as early showcases for their talent, drive, and a move to New York City or Hollywood. Even the great industrialists of the past and the corporate giants of today have similarities in hobbies, methods, interests, habits, and lifestyles.

Remember, you live in a different era. You're not so much trying to emulate what these people did as look for *patterns* and see what methods have contributed to their success, as well as what hasn't worked. Recognize also the element of chance and luck. They couldn't totally control fads and trends, or people's reactions to them (though Madonna has come very close). Many people succeed because they offer the right thing at the right time—an occurrence that always looks much easier in hindsight. Obviously, the robber barons such as Rockefeller, Carnegie, and Vanderbilt capitalized on the industrial revolution in America and were required to pay little in taxes compared with corporations of today. Frank Sinatra appealed to and influenced the young music purchasers of the 1940s as Garth Brooks and Ice-T do today. The nineties are experiencing the return of the "Buy American" movement, popular in the seventies. Learn from others and incorporate the information into your own life and plans without trying to follow in their footsteps.

People are one of the richest resources for the development of your career. Make sure you are basing career decisions on the most solid firsthand information you can possibly gather. Not hearsay. Not fantasy. And not with rigid goals in mind.

9

Planning for College and Considering Graduate School

Obviously, your preparation is going to include becoming qualified and knowledgeable in your field. This chapter will discuss how to get the most effective use of your formal education.

Education: What It Can and Can't Do for You

Today college is too costly to be a place to go in order to "find yourself." Of course, salaries have increased as the cost of living has gone up, but certainly not 200 percent in the past twenty-five years—especially starting salaries—as has the cost of college tuition. Twenty-five years ago it was possible to go to a good state school for a few hundred dollars a year. An average private college or university cost a bit more than a thousand dollars a year. Now a community college can run several thousand dollars, while a top school costs more than twenty thousand dollars a year.

Whereas college study used to be aimed at gaining exposure to many different types of subjects, it has now become a costly investment in your future. For many, college was a way of marking time before entering the real world, or perhaps just a big playground in which to enjoy beer blasts.

When deciding about investing in a formal education, ask yourself this: *Does my dream job require more education or a specific type of experience that I don't have?* Only by finding out what's required or preferred can you make informed choices about how to round off your educational experience.

The purpose of college is to educate yourself in the areas that will prepare you for the career of your choice. However, it should also be a place for personal and intellectual development. Is college necessary to succeed? Yes, but ... We all know people who have succeeded without college, and some people just aren't cut out for it at all. Still, it may be a necessity to enter certain fields at any level. For other areas where it's not utterly necessary, the added dimension of a college degree can improve your road to advancement and lead to promotions much more quickly.

Obviously, the greatest concern if you choose not to pursue higher education is, "What if I need it later on?" As indicated earlier, people change careers now more than they used to. Also, what if you think you want to be an excavator for your whole life, which doesn't require a degree, and later decide you want to be a manager at a construction company, where a degree *is* required? Or what if you *did* go to college, but since you were clueless about what you should study, you took Classical Civilization because it was fun. A knowledge of ancient Roman government is probably not the degree the construction company had in mind. The bottom line is: Don't specialize in something you don't plan on pursuing. Stick with liberal arts or take a year to try some different jobs before choosing a major.

If you have little direction and are just entering college, it might be prudent to take a year off and work at different jobs. If you've been attending school continuously since that first day of kindergarten, it might be wise to let your brain refuel for awhile. At worst, you can eliminate those things in which you don't want to be involved.

Taking time off between high school and college is considered a perfectly valid choice by most future employers and by schools themselves. The four-years-in-a-row-right-after-high-school path is no longer *de rigueur*. Some people don't start their freshman year until they're twenty-five . . . and you can bet they get more out of their classes and make better use of opportunities in college than their "undecided" eighteen-year-old counterparts.

Therefore, it's best to be really ready, to have some idea of what you want to pursue, *before* committing the time and money, or taking out loans to fund your education. This does not mean setting ultimate goals but instead using college to delve into the different fields that have sparked your interest and determine for sure where your niche is. Don't walk out with a degree until you're sure.

College can be a forgiving place for false starts. If you start with anthropology and realize it's not for you, then try your next preference. If religious studies bore you to death, then switch to philosophy. If that doesn't work, try political science. Again, it is more common than not to change your major several times, even in senior year—or even to transfer to several different schools before you find an academic home. (I started out taking summer classes at the University of Buffalo, then enrolled at the University of Michigan, dropped out, and later switched to New York University.)

Don't settle on a campus until you find one that's comfortable and stimulating. Once again, do some research and consult guides to four-year colleges, two-year colleges, or competitive colleges to get a good profile of different institutions. Most schools are very strong in some academic areas and weak in others. You don't want to attend a school that allocates no money to your area of interest.

Also consider overall costs. Maybe you can get the same quality faculty, courses, reputation, and environment for a better price. Consult *Money* magazine's annual roundup of the top one hundred schools for your money, which includes information on how to get the best deal on financial aid.

Likewise, don't settle on a major until you find something that *grabs* you. Majoring in economics does *not* mean taking the required courses and trying to get A's. It means figuring out all the possibilities an economics degree opens up to you, whether you would enjoy working in any of them, and if you would be *good* at them. *The Occupational Outlook Handbook* lists the requirements for each occupation, including what type of degree is necessary, what majors are acceptable, and any qualifying examinations.

I'm not suggesting that you have to study only the most practical subjects. Let's go back to our Ancient Civilization example. If this topic is what excites you, you *will* find a way to use your knowledge and degree to pursue a fulfilling career. It might be more difficult than walking out with a psychology degree, and may not pay as much, but there are ways to parlay any interest into a job. And if it's money you're after, it is certainly possible to combine some entrepreneurial ideas with your interest in ancient civilization, whether it be starting a museum or taking groups (maybe stressed-out accountants) on digs to Egypt. If you don't have any business skills, don't worry. Many people with business know-how are waiting to team up with a person who has a good idea and the working knowledge to back it up. Let them complete the brochures, bank accounts, legal filings, and so on.

If you've chosen to be a professional, such as a doctor, lawyer, veterinarian, physicist, or architect, any of which obviously take considerable training, then it is *imperative* to work in the field before making such a commitment. Work as an intern, office assistant, or volunteer. You would be surprised at the number of people who earn their degrees as professionals and are dissatisfied with, and even surprised by, the type of work they have undertaken. The stock exchange had more than a handful of bored lawyers and doctors who took early retirement, and engineers who were dissatisfied with their pay scale. These people had spent considerable money and an enormous amount of time on education, only to leave their professions because they were unfulfilled. Career experience is never a waste, because of the insights you gain and the things you learn. But these folks certainly spent a number of unhappy years trying to muster the courage or money to change directions.

One more warning: Even when you feel certain of your path or your major, you still have to shape the education experience to your own needs. Lily Tomlin used to perform a funny stand-up comedy routine as Ernestine, the telephone operator, mocking AT&T in the days when it had a monopoly on phone service. The premise was that all of the phone company's systems and services were available to anyone who could figure out how to use them—if one could get past the phone company's efforts to thwart its customers with inconvenience bordering on harassment. Ernestine's tag line went, "Here at the phone company we handle 84 billion calls a year, serving everyone from presidents and kings to the scum of the earth. We don't care. We don't have to. We're the phone company."

It's pretty much the same with high school, college, graduate school, and other educational programs; all the tools are there, operators (instructors, administrators and counselors) are standing by, but no one can decide on a career for you. After you have acquired these skills, there is no set way to proceed or direction to follow with your career. But as a bureaucratic body, the educational establishment really doesn't care. It's not their job to care.

Realize that schools across the country are cloning you. For the most part, you're being taught the same information from the same books and taking the same tests as millions of other students. *You're* the one who has to figure out a way to use your schooling and get ideas, abilities, and experiences out of it that everyone else isn't. It's your job to personalize the education factory in a way that will give you an edge, and an advantage in starting your career. Use every means you can think of to expand your education into a source of practical experience. You can work in your school's administrative offices or do research for professors; you can also work at the sports center or in the health services offices; you can book campus events or be a musician at fraternity parties. Take advantage of access to guest lecturers, special-interest groups, trips, and political organizations.

At a small school, if they don't offer a course you want, you might be able to find a professor interested in forming a small seminar. Some schools also let you tailor your own program—creating a self-designed, combined, or double major built around a theme— or offer multidisciplinary majors focused on a specific topic, such as urban studies.

What to Study

Don't choose your courses based strictly on what is going to be "useful" or economically rewarding, (law, investment banking) or provide job security (nursing, accounting). Marine biology may not be your calling, but if it sounds exciting, a class in oceanography may be very stimulating and give you new insights and ideas. The only useless classes are ones in which you are uninterested or for which you don't have much ability. Obviously, some core courses cannot be avoided, but if class after class in your major is a turn-off, it might be time to reevaluate your pursuit of that particular degree.

If you go through a four-year program and take the first offer that comes your way without advancing your own search, you're severely limiting your options at a time when it could make a lifetime difference. Make full use of job banks, on-campus interviews (job fairs), advisers, placement officers, school-sponsored internships for credit, work/study programs, and independent studies to explore areas not covered in the curriculum. Professors can be a great source of contacts and opportunities, so make use of their office hours to bounce ideas off them.

Should You Take an Advanced Degree?

It's a myth that additional school can "never hurt in the long run." Like college, graduate school probably won't cause a lot of physical pain, but it can certainly eat up a large portion of your income and be a big waste of time if your heart is not in what you are studying.

Does the job you eventually want require a graduate degree? If not, the extra credentials might wind up making you look more expensive to a company.

And the extra time necessary for school could have been spent gaining experience in your field and working your way up the ladder.

However, a graduate degree *can* give you added flexibility. For example, an undergraduate degree in art history and a graduate degree in public administration could be just the right combination to run a gallery or museum. A bachelor's in music with a master's in marketing might give you a better chance at being a talent agent or producing rock videos.

Do some research before you take the plunge into postgraduate studies. If you owe money on undergraduate loans, maybe this is a chance to start getting caught up financially. In fact, student-loan collection agencies have ways of finding you anywhere, even a campsite at Yellowstone Park. (The people who put the photographs on milk cartons would have a much higher recovery rate if they teamed up with the student-loan crew.)

Definitely do an internship in the area you plan to study, if you haven't had any hands-on experience. Even if it isn't a formal internship of a specified length where you will receive some type of credit or remuneration, be creative and find a way to volunteer for at least a week or two.

If you're positive that graduate school is necessary, try to land some type of job in your field of study. Be aware of the Job Bank Series, which comprises eighteen books containing extensive and up-to-date employment information on hundreds of the largest employers in each job market. Each book in the series is keyed to a specific city, and is updated annually. Each listing includes whom to call, where to write, and what to ask. Even if it's an assistant or entry-level position, ask if the company will pay for or contribute something toward your tuition. Many companies can get a tax write-off for most of the tuition if it directly relates to the business in which they are involved. Maybe you can charge graduate school to Uncle Sam. Your local bookstore should carry *The Government Job Finder*, which lists 1,400 sources of vacancies for professionals, labor, trade, technical, and office staff in the United States and overseas that are not found in the classifieds. Also included are specifics on how to prepare your cover letter and resumé, and how to interview.

If the company won't pay for school, it's still a good idea to work in the field you are studying. Lectures and books will be all the more meaningful when applied to real problems and situations. Also, it gets some of the initial drudgery—learning your way around, understanding systems and policies—out of the way, as well as providing a great source of contacts and networking for seeking the job for which you will soon be qualified.

On a lighter note: If you would like to be more educated, but don't feel like taking the time or spending the money; if you are ambitious but don't want to do the necessary research and legwork; or if you want to be on top without working your way up, get a copy of *How to Start Your Own Country*, by Erwin S. Strauss. Of special interest are the chapters on recruiting settlers and the future of new countries.

10

Work for Free

The Importance of Experience

Once you've found something you might be interested in pursuing, try some hands-on experience. Fortunately, many businesses, professions, and activities require a support staff—whether it's the person who directs traffic at an excavation site, does the bookkeeping, stands by the net under the trapeze at the circus, or answers the phones. If you want to fight forest fires, what could be better than having a part-time job at a ranger station? If your goal is to be a publicist, then working as a receptionist at a public-relations firm is an ideal starting point.

Unfortunately, matches like this don't always happen; the position is not usually open when you're looking for it. If you don't have any connections with people already in the business, you don't have a competitive advantage. And of course, if you don't know anyone in that particular business, then you probably don't have any experience in it, which makes you even less desirable from the business's point of view. It's really a vicious circle. Most employers are also going to avoid someone who is just looking at the job as a short-term steppingstone to something better, because then they are wasting company resources in processing and training you, just to have to repeat the procedure in a few months. So, when you are experimenting in different career environments, it's often necessary to *offer your services free of charge.*

Before you balk at this suggestion and insist that you're "worth" a certain sum and would never allow yourself to be exploited, consider the advantages: You don't have to commit yourself to a period of time, and you don't have to feel that you've disappointed anyone by bailing out after just a week if you think this job was a mistake. If it *does* work out, you will have experience and will make a better-qualified candidate for a paid position in the future, a definite resumé enhancement. If you make a good impression, you'll also have an employer to list as a reference.

The main objective in working for free is to avoid committing time and money to training for a career in which you don't have a clear idea of the actual work. You are drawing a road map for the rest of your life. Just as progress increases the rewards, making changes and alterations becomes more expensive with every additional mile. Now is the time to concentrate on what will make a challenging work life, not the first day on the job.

Working for free doesn't mean quitting the job you already have, or working for free on a full-time basis. You can do as little as contact people and politely interview them about their businesses, arrange to work part-time, or develop an internship.

Developing an Internship

An internship is basically an exchange of work for knowledge. Some internships pay a small stipend, which might cover your transportation expenses, but most do not pay anything at all. Occasionally they offer small perks such as free meals, use of company facilities, or tickets to concerts or events. However, working for free is actually quite profitable if you take the time to figure out how much money it costs every time you sit down in a classroom seat in school, whether it's being funded by tax dollars or tuition.

Internships are *required* in many fields, such as teaching, social work, law, and medicine. In Washington, D.C., an internship (usually with very low pay) is almost the only entry into a political career. Some colleges are even sponsoring programs that give academic credit for jobs in D.C. Otherwise, the Senate Placement Office counsels applicants and refers resumés. The House Placement Office operates a similar service. For outsiders, an entry-level position is the only way to gain access to people and subsequent jobs.

Many publications have internships for aspiring journalists. For many years, Time Warner has invited college juniors and graduate students to Manhattan to work at *Time* and *Life* magazines, as well as in other facets of their publishing enterprise.

To seek an internship in standard fields such as communications, creative arts, human services, public affairs, science, business, etc., consult *Peterson's Guide to Internships,* published annually. It should be available at the library, a bookstore, or a career center, or you can order it from Peterson's Guides. This guide describes about 38,000 short-term job opportunities in twenty-three career fields. Each listing gives you the contact, a description of duties, necessary qualifications, availability of college credit, pay or fringe benefits, and long-term job possibilities. Also included is a list of overseas internship opportunities.

Surprisingly, a lot of employers, workers, and professionals don't understand the concept of internship. They think they have to build a school adjacent to corporate headquarters, that it has to do with day care, or that they will have to administer exams. Be aware of the differences between a standard intern program such as you'd find at a corporation like General Mills or a large financial company such as Merrill Lynch, versus a local outfit run by just four or five people, or an unusual place such as a horse-training farm or an auction house, where it isn't likely that any such program would exist. Prepare yourself to sell the idea to them.

In a corporate environment where new interns arrive every six months, full-time employees get burned out on eager faces anxious to learn. If, however, you apply at the kind of place that has never had an intern and you can work out an arrangement, you'll probably have an even better experience than you would in a program with many others. In a smaller-scale outfit, the other workers will be more likely to treat you as an employee, fully explain the job, and allow you to actually try things.

The Do-It-Yourself Program

You need some initiative and creativity to be the first intern, whether it's at the local pediatrician's office or with the superintendent of a school system. First, make a list of all your capabilities. It should include the following (with a few of your own talents thrown in such as typing or driving—which makes you available for errands—or knowledge in a specific area):

- Basic bookkeeping (this doesn't mean accounting or require any complicated math, usually just tallying up receipts or expenses).
- Answering phones, taking messages, giving out information such as dates, times, and places of events with which the business is involved.

- Running errands, getting lunches, making coffee, restocking supplies.
- Photocopying, filing, collating, mailing. Any computer skills help in this area.
- Answering inquiries by mail.
- Assisting people working on projects that just require an extra set of hands to perform simple tasks.

All of the above skills are valuable to almost any organization or business. Are there other skills you can add to the list—for example, proofreading, word processing, computer programming, researching, repairing, or drawing? Can you make travel arrangements, organize events, build things, set up displays, or make models?

Next, make a "hit list" of places to try. In many instances your options will be geographically limited. If you want to drive racing cars or be on a pit crew, and there is only one track in the area, that's the only place to go. This is the time to really brainstorm. If you've always wondered what it would be like to work as a blacksmith or a gemologist, consult *Dun's Regional Business Directories* along with those Yellow Pages.

Small start-ups and one-on-one situations are ideal for taking responsibility and wearing many different hats. If the place isn't familiar with internships, then maybe that's not even a good word to use when approaching them. You might want to use the term "volunteer" or "unpaid apprentice." Just explain that you want to work for free in exchange for hands-on experience because you are interested in this area and are thinking about pursuing it as a career. Explain your skills, along with the fact that you would enjoy learning any other specific jobs you might be able to perform (for example, if given the sales pitch, maybe you could phone potential clients).

Set out a reasonable time frame such as two or three weeks of full-time work or six weeks of part-time work. Be assured that if the internship works out, the organization will be glad to have you stay as long as you would like. (If they're shorthanded, that's usually the time to ask to be put on the payroll.) Likewise, if things don't work out, either of you can end the arrangement as early as necessary.

One other good preparation is to forge an academic connection, in case the employer is skeptical of your motives, concerned that you won't have much commitment, or reluctant to deviate from standard employment procedures and hours. (Be prepared: A lot of people will think you're off your rocker to work for free.) If you're in *any* type of education program — high school, college, or trade school — then go to a professor, adviser, or guidance counselor and see if there is any way to receive credit or be "sponsored" by the school.

This can mean as little as talking to a teacher about the work you are going to do and asking if he or she will act as a reference for you, in exchange for which you can write a paper on the experience, if necessary. It seems like a silly enough arrangement, but now when you approach this company, group, hospital, or whatever, your proposal will sound very academic and educational. If you've ever watched students selling lottery tickets, taking surveys, or getting signatures for petitions, you may have noticed that passersby are always more eager to help a student. They feel it's a good cause, and, recalling their own experience as students, might have a soft spot for other students. Now, if need be, your approach can include the statement, "I'm a student," or "I'm working on a project for such-and-such school with Professor so-and-so."

Explain to those whom you approach that you

are considering entering the type of business they are in and would like to gain some relevant experience before committing yourself with education, full-time work, and so on. If one person is not qualified to help you, he or she should be able to put you in touch with someone who can. In the end, it's hard to resist someone who is enthusiastic enough to work for nothing.

Making Free Work Pay Off

Treat this opportunity as a regular job by showing up for work on time and fulfilling any responsibilities assigned to you. Keep a notebook and jot down things you don't understand but will have to look up or ask someone to explain later. Also, keep a log of all that you accomplish or tasks you complete.

Make sure you introduce yourself to all the people you will be working with, and explain that you are trying to learn about the work they do. This will make it easy to ask a question or two at appropriate times. *Don't* ask about information that may be considered sensitive (e.g., client lists, sales techniques, salaries, or commissions) in a competitive work environment such as direct sales, agenting, or telemarketing.

Familiarize yourself with any computer software or office procedures which could enable you to increase the parameters of your job functions. Don't wait to be given directions if you have run out of projects. Ask people if there is anything you can do to help them, and make suggestions. Can you do some typing, mailing, or errand-running? Can you update lists, pick up something in the cafeteria, cross-index a Rolodex, make copies, or do word processing?

How to Finance Working for Free

Investments in the future usually result in present sacrifices, whether it's diminished leisure time, personal budget cuts, or working at unpleasant tasks. Take the usual shortcuts where you can find them — staying close to home, working on weekends, and seeking out low-cost entertainment.

Do some work in as many of your interest areas as you can, even if it's making a one-day visit to a company, taking a factory tour, or accepting a volunteer position. Use time after school or work, or on weekends or during vacations. These career explorations don't necessarily have to be aimed at your dream job, but just something about which you always wondered, such as being a metallurgist or an interior decorator. Or perhaps you've always thought it would be exciting to work at a zoo, a science center, or a marina. Well, investigate. Once again, if it's something you enjoy, it shouldn't feel like work!

It may take years of work and study, a lot of effort, and many mistakes to find something you truly love to do. However, the time spent eliminating certain vocations is certainly not to be considered a waste of time.

Some people naturally fall into a job or a profession. They've wanted to do that type of work since they were five, and are quite content to go to school and eventually take their place in the work world. If you're not one of them — or even if you are — don't stop seeking your niche and settle for a college major or a career that doesn't stimulate you, just because it offers "security." You're going to be bored and wishing it were Friday until the day you turn sixty-five.

Making the Most of Your "Internship"

Once you're ensconced in an internship, look for signals indicating that you're on the right track. This could mean that you don't realize how quickly the time goes by when you are working, or you leave the work feeling invigorated and refreshed. Another indication is that your mind is stimulated to think of the work in your spare time (and not about how stressed out you are) because of the genuine interest in what you are doing. It's at this critical point of success that most people stop and become satisfied that they are content to do a certain type of work, instead of activating their career entrepreneur mode.

Having a passion for something is just a part of the process. In your unpaid job—just as in an established, lucrative career—it's not so much *attitude* as *action* that counts.

• *Talk to Everyone You Can Corner.* Use this opportunity to continue exchanging views and information with other people in the business you're interested in entering. Find out from them about seminars, courses, and lectures, or read trade papers and the local or nearest city newspaper. Have business cards printed just so you can ask to exchange phone numbers with someone easily. (They are an excellent investment and usually cost under twenty dollars for five hundred.) Even if you don't have a title or a steady salaried position, just get a plain white standard card with black printing that has your name in the middle with your address and phone number(s) in the corners. If you're away at school, just put your dorm or apartment phone number and home phone number (with area codes!) as you would do on a resumé.

• *Don't Just Do the Work You're Assigned.* Think of new projects that will improve the business and get permission to implement them. Everybody has at least some good ideas, but few act on them. Many people don't try hard enough or long enough to follow through, get the necessary information, and make contacts with people who can help them. Working for free is the perfect opportunity to experiment with such new and better ideas. You've got the resources at hand (equipment, location, people—whatever constitutes your workplace), yet if you "fail," no permanent harm is done. In a sense, you're just performing an experiment and accumulating learning experiences. So what if the boss says you're crazy? It's not going in your personnel file, because you don't have one yet.

Say you're trying out working in a transportation company. Your idea may be as simple an improvement as computerizing the employees' Rolodexes at work, or a full-blown scheme such as starting and marketing a bus or ferryboat service for tired automobile commuters. Take advantage of your fledgling status to propose new ideas. You could help yourself and your company.

Let's go back to the project of computerizing Rolodexes. Some employees won't want to change their system even if it will save them time and energy. Your plan should be to present the project in a way that makes it seem desirable for people to learn the new system, maybe by inputting one employee's list of clients and contacts into the computer and using this as a demonstration (especially if you're the one who's been updating all the mailing lists).

You may have to update the software in order to get the most efficient program. And of course you'll have to show everyone how to access the information, and make a typed list of instructions for all employees to keep on their desks until they're completely familiar with the new system. Yes, it's going to require thought and effort and risk.

However . . . if you do have a viable plan and have

the motivation, confidence, and ambition to do your homework and put it into action, you'll likely meet with success. This could lead to a job offer, or at least a great addition to your resumé. If you initiate such a project in your preexisting job, you'll become a greater asset to your employer and co-workers, who should eventually reward you with a promotion. (A few corporations even give bonuses for new ideas and methods.) And don't stop there. After successfully putting one improvement into action, your mind should already be working on the next one.

If it's a really big entrepreneurial project you've launched—such as a bike shop, a new magazine, or a restaurant—you'll find that venture capitalists (investors who fund new ideas) are like good employers in that they are ready to support people with determination and ideas, not just products. Of course, they'll want a cut of the profits when you succeed.

• *Plot a More Specific Course for the Future. Now* is the time to set a flexible goal. What, specifically, do you want to do in this business? What position best matches your skills? What will it take to get there? Additional study? Apprenticeship? Working extra hours? If you want to be a leader in your field, it is probably a good idea to be proficient at every aspect of the job, so when you have mastered one area in your "internship" (or, for that matter, in your current job), try to get involved in learning something else. Don't just keep doing what you do best.

If you want to manage and train others, for example, it is best to have a broad background, having worked at every job yourself at one time—or at least to be familiar with all the processes involved. Say you're interested in publishing and have chosen manuscript evaluation as your area of interest. Just for perspective, talk to the people in the legal, sales, advertising, production, art, and administrative departments. These discussions will give depth to your understanding and possibly act as a springboard for new ideas.

Use other volunteering activities separate from your internship or job to enlarge your skills and broaden your perspectives. For example, when I was a teenager, volunteering to run charity auctions definitely honed my skills to be a Wall Street trader by forcing me to think on my feet. On the other hand, organizing church rummage sales has kept me out of the secondhand clothing and discount furniture businesses. For you, volunteer work might mean doing PR or fund-raising for educational, religious, charitable, artistic, or political groups.

Whatever way you choose to get involved, volunteer work will provide a means of widening acquaintances and polishing your organizational and decision-making skills. It will also let you experience an egalitarian workplace. When you are planning events with other volunteers, the salary stigma is removed and your input is on equal terms with others. You needn't battle the hierarchy most of us encounter at our jobs. This creates an opportunity to "show your stuff" unfettered. Community volunteer work also happens to look great on resumés, counts as experience, and can provide recommendations and maybe job leads.

Working for free is about taking chances, experimenting with different types of work and meeting people until it eventually pays off with experience, knowledge, or a job opportunity. Hockey player Wayne Gretzky once reported that he had a coach who complained of his lack of scoring in an important game. The coach made his point by saying, "You miss one hundred percent of the shots you never take."

11

Finding a Job

Getting Your Foot in the Door

It's just as important to be entrepreneurial in how you land an actual position as it is when you're already on the job. Don't wait to be "picked" for a certain career as a result of following normal job-hunting channels and processes such as answering ads or making the rounds of available job interviews. Being "picked" happens when all the initiative is exercised by the employer and not by the job applicant; you're reduced to trying to prove to each new stony-faced interviewer that you are whatever he or she wants you to be. Moreover, normal job-hunting procedures such as listing with agencies and answering want ads are often insufficient, especially when the economy is poor.

First, shore up your resources. If your resumé is lousy, then redo it. Get one of the many books on the subject, such as *The Resumé Catalog: 200 Damn Good Examples* by Yana Parker, and figure out how to make your job at the drive-through Kodak booth look as though it was a job in film production. If you can't write a cover letter, find out how, or find someone who can! If you tend to crack during interviews, then practice with friends, tape yourself with a camcorder, and invest in a how-to book such as *Sweaty*

Palms: The Neglected Art of Being Interviewed, by H. Anthony Medley. In other words, address your weaknesses and improve on them.

Next, contact people and companies for whom you want to work, but who may not be looking for someone right now. Indicate that you're waiting for something to open up. If you can head a company off at the pass by putting your name up for a job that won't be available for another six months, you might save them from advertising the position (expensive) and interviewing other candidates (time-consuming). This does not mean bombarding them with calls and resumés each week, but rather nurturing some relationships to re-contact periodically until you can find a permanent way into their working arena (maybe even with some more "working for free.")

Most jobs are secured through networking. But let's face it—often you just don't know anyone who can help you. If you haven't been able to make the right contacts through your research, friends, teachers, and so on, but you are sure of what you want to do, it may be best to lower your expectations temporarily by taking an entry-level or "grunt" position (if you've already done internships) and working your way up. Or you can work for free as much as possible while holding another job—say, as a waitress or grocery clerk—in order to make the necessary contacts and get to know people.

There are some arguments for taking one of the first jobs that comes along:

• If you don't get the money rolling in soon, you may be faced with indefinite unemployment or settling for a position in which you are low-paid.

• If you continue to interview because this job is not very appealing, it puts you in a stronger position with a potential employer; he won't be wondering why no one has hired you, and he'll know you are capable of holding a full-time position.

There are also several disadvantages:

• It's difficult to continue the job-search process, and it's unfair to your present employer, if you are devoting your work time to that pursuit. And having worked only a few months for one employer doesn't look great on a resumé.

• It doesn't make a very good impression to leave a job after just two weeks because you found a better position. It's not the best way to gain a recommendation.

Use your judgment according to how difficult it is to enter your field, how many jobs are available, and how often they arise. If you know it could take you a while to get the situation you desire, then work in the meantime. You can tell your employer in a polite way that you have certain goals and have trained yourself to accept a certain level of responsibility and are interested in a specific field. It's possible that in the long run your employer could actually help you to find the position you seek.

Even if you are working at a job that is far beneath your skill and educational level, if you have a positive attitude and work attentively, you will likely be the first person considered when a position in which you're interested opens up. (Don't assume anything, however; you still have to win the job against other outside applicants.) Many companies, though committed to "promotion from within," are legally bound to advertise job openings to the public at large. Then again, if you've made a point of getting to know and impress many people, you may be offered the job while interviewing proceeds simply as a formality.

In the meantime, and without making too much of the fact that you are doing work that is "beneath you," make sure that fellow employees are aware that you have training and aspire to move up when an opportunity presents itself. Just don't pose a threat to other skilled workers who are content with their work, but may not have the same level of education as you do.

Obviously, some jobs require certain degrees, licenses, or connections even to obtain an interview. Many job searches require a resumé and subsequent interviewing. If you don't have these qualifications and tools, there is no "back door" to enter through in order to secure those types of positions. Even if you did a fantastic job of delivering your neighbor's baby in the back of a taxicab on the way to the hospital, no hospital is going to let you repeat the performance. Licenses are required for everything from styling hair and driving a bus to selling flowers as a street vendor. In most cities you can't even offer to perform plumbing or electrical work without licenses, permits, and union membership. In other words, approach the organizations you've picked only after you're sure you have the qualifications to offer services they need.

Locating Employers
It is important to explore every avenue of the job market. So whether you are trying to find entry-level work or skilled or unskilled labor, or to open your own business, exploit these opportunities. Locate and try to contact every company, business, organization, or employer for whom you might consider working. Be prepared to spend many hours in the library taking

notes, and many more following up. If it takes under a hundred hours to research job possibilities, then you've cheated yourself. When you accept a position, do it knowing that you have secured as many offers as you possibly could at this particular time.

If you have a great entrepreneurial idea—a new cereal, board game, or children's toy—consider going to work for a company in that field instead of trying to start out on your own. It's more efficient to utilize existing structures than to start from scratch with limited experience your first time out. In an official role at an established company, you'll gain training and experience in marketing, patenting, design, financial and legal considerations, and distribution, among other things. Maybe you'll improve upon your idea and pursue it on the side, decide it wasn't as viable as you first thought, or end up sharing it with your employers in exchange for some type of compensation. Why risk failing with a good idea just because you lack a good foundation of knowledge and procedures to launch your project? Besides, you're going to have a lot more good ideas!

Taking these pointers into consideration, it's time to develop your plan of attack: Target your potential employers and pinpoint the people in a position to hire you.

Develop an international list of possible employers from the following sources, all of which can be found at a large central library:

• *Standard and Poor's Register of Corporations, Directors and Executives*

• *Moody's Industrial Manual*

• *Value Line Investment Survey*

• *Who's Who in Finance and Industry*

• *Dun's Directory of Service Companies* (lists information on accessing the fifty thousand largest service companies)

• *The Million Dollar Directory* (provides detailed information on more than 160,000 of America's largest companies, both public and private, and includes key facts on decision-makers)

• *Fortune* magazine's compilation of the top five hundred companies

• *Forbes's* annual list of successful small companies

• Newspaper, trade paper, and magazines articles and advertisements you've been filing

• Newspaper classifieds (get out-of-town and even international papers such as the *Financial Times*)

• Yellow Pages (obtain phone books from areas where you would like to work by calling the phone company in that city) for access to small companies (employing from two to twenty-five people), specialty jobs, such as animal trainers, and service providers, such as chimney sweepers and landscapers

Don't limit your search to a particular town, state, or country, especially if you are just beginning and don't have family responsibilities. Expecting to find all great career possibilities in one place (preferably within a twenty-minute commute from your home) isn't realistic. Be open-minded enough to go where the work is for now. Down the line, when you've begun to be successful, you'll have more chances to choose where you'll live.

For a guide to employment agencies, send for the *National Directory of Personnel Consultants* which lists agencies by state, city, and job specialization. It's available in some libraries.

If you are fluent in a foreign language, consider working in another country. Or if you are not, there are always Australia and the United Kingdom. (Given the current state of their economies, an unskilled laborer will not be as welcome as someone who can contribute specific skills or experience.) However, more and more Americans without knowledge of any other language are successfully working in countries such as Sweden, Japan, Germany, Switzerland, and the Netherlands, where a great deal of English is spoken. In Singapore and Hong Kong, much business is transacted in English. It's possible to avoid visa problems and protectionist laws that discourage hiring foreigners if you work for an American-based firm that has offices overseas, or for a multinational corporation or agency.

International career opportunities can be found in the federal government, the United Nations, international banking, management consulting, political risk analysis, nonprofit organizations, international business, journalism, publishing, communications, teaching, and international law. More summer jobs are offered by the federal government than by any industry; it has a policy of attracting young talent. However, most are for those with some type of background in economics, public administration, or business administration. These are listed in the *Federal Jobs Digest*, a bi-monthly publication which can be subscribed to and can be found at your local public library.

If you are interested in pursuing international work, read periodicals such as *World Link, World Trade, Far Eastern Economic Review,* and *International Business.* These magazines provide valuable, up-to-date information about the fastest-growing companies, industries and markets. You can find leads to jobs and ideas in the profiles, ads, classified sections, and reviews of other literature on the international marketplace. The *Directory of Overseas Summer Jobs* is also worth looking at, along with *The Complete Guide to International Jobs and Careers* by Ron and Caryl Krannick. If you have a special objective, read *International Jobs: Where They Are and How to Get Them,* by Eric Kocher. It lists five hundred career opportunities around the world, with specific information on qualifications, resumés, and available publications.

By the way, packing up and working in a new place is an adventure that does not appeal to most people. After a few years in an area, especially if you've just gotten married, started a family, or purchased a house, even a promotional transfer can be considered an inconvenience. When an opportunity to work in a foreign country for a one- or two-year assignment comes up, not as many people as you might think are interested in taking it. Even fewer are prepared to commit themselves to moving indefinitely. So if you have the spirit, you're more likely to get the assignment.

Making Contact

After you've narrowed down your employer candidates, your next step is to contact them. However, sending a cover letter and a resumé "To Whom It May Concern" is not going to do the trick. Start by calling the company and getting in touch with the personnel or human resources department, or whatever they call it. Don't even start your calls, though, until you're sure that you know what the company does and what type of position you are ideally interested in getting. When you call, ask the following questions:

• What are the job application procedures?

• Are there any openings?

• What are the qualifications?

• If nothing is available, to whom can you send your resumé and cover letter so that it will be kept on file for any future positions?

So far, this sounds simple enough. But you're seldom allowed to ask all these questions and get straight answers because the personnel department is trained like an antiaircraft missile to discourage any approach other than through conventional channels.

What you'll probably run into is this:

• Personnel department: "If you're answering an advertisement, send your resumé to whatever department was listed." (Of course, if you ask, "Where was this ad?" they probably won't tell you.)

• An attitude implying there is never going to be another opening in your lifetime, but, if you insist, you can send your resumé—though no one will look at it anyway.

• Refusal to divulge the names of any department heads whom you may want to try contacting.

Bottom line: You may have to call back a few times and try to speak with different people. (Or disguise your voice.)

A more fruitful approach is to call the switchboard and ask for a department in which you'd most likely to get a foot in the door (try marketing or PR—they're people-oriented, and almost always nice) and get hold of a receptionist or secretary. Your goal is to get as much information as possible from him or her about job prospects. (They usually know of job openings before anyone else.) See if you can speak with someone in authority, or at least obtain the name of the department head; the switchboard will sometimes tell you that.

Next, go slowly and be polite, but try for the moon. If there aren't any openings, request to ask the person a few questions about the field, or stop in for ten minutes if it's not too far away. Ask how he or she recommends you proceed in your job search. Are there any other departments in the company that you should contact? What about other companies? Can you mention this person's name when you make that contact? May you send a resumé in case something opens up? What about any part-time work? May you call back in a month? If this job is really what you want, how about discussing an internship when you call back? Always send a thank-you note. This person's time is valuable, and he or she doesn't know you from a jack-in-the-box and just did you a huge favor. At large organizations, try going through the switchboard and hitting every department. You never know when an assistant just stormed out the door. Timing can be everything.

Many career guides suggest you send a resumé and cover letter to the person who could hire you. This approach could work, especially in a small firm. But they're just as likely to be very busy, and will simply send your materials back to Personnel. It's all part of the process. The point really is, don't be afraid to call, speak to people, ask questions. Your goal is to gather names and information—*inside* information—that could give you an edge over someone who mails his paperwork into the corporate void. It's really a no-lose proposition—they don't know who you are, and you're basically in control.

Presentation

I'm not going into any more specifics about interviewing, writing cover letters, and effective resumés, because if you're motivated enough to do a great job search, these are just basic necessities. All these things are important, because if you can't look presentable for an interview, how are you going to make a good impression on co-workers and clients? If you can't take the time to write a thank-you note and compose a well-crafted cover letter, how are you going to follow up at your job? Simple stuff, but worth remembering, especially when you are getting job-search burnout and are inclined to start taking shortcuts.

However, there are some things you should do *before* speaking to a contact at a company or arriving at an interview.

1. Try to arrange your meeting for a time before or after business hours so you have a better chance of getting the person's undivided attention.

2. Research the company. If it's a public company, talk with a local stockbroker to get financial information and a good idea of what services the company provides or products it makes. You can also do this at the library, but the information won't be current. Stockbrokers have at their fingertips a lot of general information about companies. They don't keep annual reports or disclosure documents on hand (the company itself can provide you with these free of charge, upon request), but they do have reference materials listing a company's earnings, founder, size, departments, location, and clippings of any recent magazine or newspaper articles.

3. The company's own PR department should be

able to provide you with informational material, advertising, press releases, or recent articles that have been published about the organization. Caveat: These will only be flattering, so read them with a grain of salt.

4. If the company that interests you is too small to have a PR department, simply call anyone at the company and ask politely, "What is it, specifically, that your organization does?" I've done this many times, and the person on the other end will usually take a few minutes to give a detailed explanation. He or she may be concerned that you are writing an article for some publication, so you may have to make it clear that you're not a journalist.

The *wrong* time to ask this last question is at a job interview. When you have your information ahead of time, it's possible to decide which aspect of the work you find interesting. Not only will you appear knowledgeable and prepared, but you'll have more to discuss with the interviewer, rather than sitting there passively answering questions.

If the position you seek doesn't require a lot of experience, focus on satisfying the employer that you possess basic skills (filing, typing a business letter), are responsible (show up on time, take accurate messages), and can get along well with co-workers and be polite to customers and clients. Your potential employer is *not* looking for a genius who wants to overhaul the way everyone does business and upset established relationships. It's okay to inform the potential boss of your aspirations and plans to work your way up, but don't go overboard with ambitiousness. If at this particular time the company needs someone to address envelopes, answer mail, and get coffee, it doesn't benefit it to have someone who is too eager to get past that job. First, if you do advance rapidly (maybe by moving to another company), they're right back where they started, needing someone to perform the above tasks, and they've wasted time and money training you and processing you for tax purposes and possibly insurance coverage. Second, if you're smart and too eager to get ahead, there's a greater chance that you will be careless and annoy co-workers.

So always respect the employer's point of view and show interest in the job for which you are applying, instead of getting ahead of yourself. There will be plenty of time to learn about the business, and once you prove that you are competent and dependable, people will gladly give you all the responsibilities you desire.

If prospects for a full-time job in your field are not looking good, make it clear to employers that you are open to alternatives that may fit their needs. Today's businesses are more careful about hiring full-time employees because of the financial and legal responsibilities involved. Instead, they are hiring more part-time and temporary workers, as well as consultants and outside contractors. Employers often take such an opportunity to look at the kind of worker you will be, and *then* make a decision about hiring you full-time. In other cases, it may just be a matter of waiting for a position to become available. By working with the company part-time, you are already trained and available to fill the opening.

Once You're In
If the only way into your chosen field is to work your way up from the bottom, do it. Your enthusiasm and interest in the work will, in time, enable you to become firmly established. If this is truly what you

love, you'll do well, and the monetary rewards will follow. The entertainment industry is famous for this bootstrap approach. The mail rooms of many powerful agencies, studios, and production companies are filled with college graduates who have their sights set on a higher position in the company. Many Wall Street hot shots started out as runners, clerks, or trader's assistants. Besides, starting at the top does not prepare you to stay there!

Being at the bottom has tremendous advantages. You can ask smart people dumb questions. You can learn from other people's mistakes. Most important, you can take time to look around and decide what the best niche for you will be. When I got my first entry-level job on the floor of the stock exchange, I knew that I wanted to work there and that I was interested in the stock market. But I had no idea what was going on. A lot of guys were yelling, screaming, fighting, and communicating with hand signals. I didn't even know the different positions to which one could aspire—clerk, price reporter, broker, specialist, trader, and others.

By taking the opportunity, during lunch and coffee breaks, to be a kind of roving reporter, I was able to talk with people who had all those jobs and conclude that I would eventually like to be a trader. Then I was able to ask how to do it, what books to read, what the next rung on the ladder would be, what skills I needed, and what classes I should take at the nearby New York Institute of Finance. This led me to buy and read books on options trading, and eventually one of these smart people, impressed by my keen interest, did offer me a job on the next rung, as a clerk. Epilogue: It took two years of grueling hard work and being the butt of every practical joke known to man, but I got my seat on the stock exchange.

If you want to advance quickly by taking more risks, look to join new startup companies whenever possible. They are the most likely to be at the cutting edge of an entrepreneurial venture, or implementing new technology. Creativity from the ranks will be welcomed if there is a strong team spirit. Rapid growth in a company often goes hand-in-hand with rapid personal advancement. Startups are typically understaffed, owing to shoestring budgets, and thus are likely to let you assume more responsibilities and wear different hats.

Play It Safe
Sometimes you have to hide your real self. We all have a wild side and we can all feel justified in saying at one time or another, "No one understands me." It may be necessary to keep your wild side a secret when you first meet with prospective employers, associates, or workers; they should not be required to understand what makes you tick. Everybody agrees that individuality is what has helped make America successful and has garnered it more Nobel prizes than any other country. Yet you don't want to frighten a potential contact, reference, or new boss with your obvious unconventionality.

Your individuality will come out soon enough through your work and application to the problems at hand. Besides, it's important for your employer, co-workers, and partners to know that you *can* conform when necessary, just as it's unnecessary to regale everyone with your life story and ambitions. All that you want to convey for now is dependability, initiative if possible, and true interest in performing the tasks required to the best of your ability.

12

Street Smarts

Eighty percent of success is showing up.

— Woody Allen

Parting Perspectives

As I've said, being a career entrepreneur never stops! It is a project that lasts a lifetime. It will also bring a lifetime of rewards, because you will continue to search and grow, and your work will become progressively more meaningful to you.

And when you like what you do, you will draw people with your enthusiasm. Individuals will begin approaching *you* to solve problems, develop concepts, lead committees, and create strategies. Not only that, but people will start depending upon your knowledge, expertise, and energy. When that happens, you're on the way to being "indispensable," which garners advancement, respect, and self-esteem.

Here are a few concepts to bear in mind as you proceed along your entrepreneurial path:

• *Knowledge in Other Areas Will Constantly Come in Handy.* Don't let graduation from high school or college mean you'll just sigh and say, "Thank God I don't have to learn any more," and order extra cable-vision channels. Keep feeding your brain with new information and updating on the latest innovations.

Until now, you've been looking into everything that sparks your interest. Now try learning about things that didn't meet this first test. Study something that you don't especially like, but that you think might help you come up with more ideas or do your job better. Every week, buy a magazine that you wouldn't normally look at and see what new ideas you glean from it. For example, if you can't wait for the next copy of *Sports Illustrated* to arrive, browse through *Architectural Digest* or the *Harvard Review*. Be aware of the different needs people have—for instance, the kinds of products, services, or entertainment the readers of a particular magazine favor. Stop in the video store and rent some documentaries on subjects about which you know next to nothing.

• *Maintain Your Decorum.* There is a difference between persistence and obnoxiousness. Unfortunately, too many career books, advice columns, and motivational seminars advance outlandish theories about focusing on and getting what you want, much of which would probably make you look ludicrous to others. Remember, there are rules and regulations to every game, including the job hunt and the field of your choice. Utilizing all the resources and contacts available to you requires time, organization, research, and study. Lots of it. That's how you will distinguish yourself. Make use of contacts, acquaintances, and inroads you may have through prior work, but remember, there's a limit to how much you can ask of people.

• *Keep on the Move, Whether or Not Things Are Going Your Way.* Don't hibernate in the bathtub with a dog-eared copy of *When Bad Things Happen to Good People.* Put probability on your side. If you're out the door by 8:00 A.M., trying to get a job, meeting people, working for free, sooner or later *something* is going to happen. The odds are with you, and not with the person who sleeps until noon. Value all your experiences. Look around at your jobs, your friends, trips you've taken, the time you moved to a different state—all provided or were the result of new experiences at one time or another. Just by going out—to school, to a party, or proceeding through daily events—you'll find that one contact leads to another.

• *Creativity Is an Asset, But Small Innovations Also Count!* An innovation can give a new slant to an old product, a different way of offering an old service, a trendier or more high-tech advertising method, or a more efficient way of organizing office work or arranging deliveries. All can significantly enhance profits for a business. A good initial idea can then be expanded upon or modified to be incorporated into your job. Remember, there are no geniuses who can't be beaten with hard work and a good idea.

• *Develop Habits that Encourage You to Use Your Talents, Face Challenges, and Be Productive.* Make sure that your lifestyle lends itself to meeting responsibilities and accepting new experiences. But there's no guaranteed formula for that, such as making a "Things to Do" list every night, or starting off with an exercise regimen each morning. For most people, the best routine is none at all. Doing things at different times in slightly different ways can make even repetitive tasks seem fresh and new. Spontaneity and flexibility are just as important to your career as military-style discipline.

Thoughts on "Success"

Keep an open mind about the meaning of success. It doesn't necessarily mean money, expensive suits, and a fancy car. Success really means achieving your goals and being happy with what you do. Besides, if you are doing something you enjoy, there are plenty of ways to make money.

Also, big-time, conventional success involves many trade-offs. If you know someone who is making huge amounts of money and think that you would readily switch places with him or her, ask yourself:

• Is this person happy?

• Would I find this job gratifying?

• What sacrifices has the person made to get where he or she is? Lots of travel? Long hours? Stress? Little time with family and friends? Lots of financial risk? Hard physical labor? Tedious, repetitive work?

Now examine the pros and cons of the whole situation before making a judgment. Believe me, you're better off as a happy, skilled tree surgeon earning a moderate income than as the miserable, overworked CPA you would have been if you'd listened to your mother.

You must have the courage of your convictions; success is often failure overcome by persistence.

• Henry Ford went broke five times before he finally succeeded.

• Eighteen publishers turned down Richard Bach's story *Jonathan Livingston Seagull* before one finally accepted it. By 1975 it had sold more than 7 million copies in the United States alone.

• The novel *M*A*S*H*, by Richard Hooker, was rejected by twenty-one publishers before Morrow picked it up.

• Baseball legend Babe Ruth, famous for setting the home-run record (851), also holds the record for strike-outs (1,030).

• Ray Kroc (McDonald's founder) didn't sell a single hamburger until he was fifty-two years old.

A Few Words on "Failure"

Entrepreneurs solve problems. And the same problem-solving techniques you apply in the business arena you must also apply to yourself, because life is never easy. Your career is going to have downs as well as ups; take them in stride as part of the process. Problem-solving in itself requires continual frustration and failure. If the answer comes too easily, it usually means that some important component was overlooked.

Instead, let yourself be stimulated by adversity. Innovation and ingenuity often result from being thrust into a situation in need of improvement. Motivation and ambition should be stronger in the person determined to change and improve his or her circumstances than in a blandly contented individual.

If you strive to achieve fulfillment, don't allow yourself to use the obstacles in your life as excuses for not being successful. Most people have had a number of difficult situations to deal with or overcome in their lives: injuries, financial woes, divorce. And if things don't work as well as planned, resist attributing your lack of success to these earlier disadvantages, and concluding that "for someone who started behind the eight ball, this should be good enough."

Moreover, for some reason, it is always easier to see why other people have a better shot at succeeding than you do. They have enjoyed better circumstances or more advantages, and it appears they have fewer obstacles before them. However, they most likely have problems you never realized, and your situation isn't as bad as you thought.

In fact, when we decide to settle for our seemingly prescribed lot in life, excuses abound: adversity, shyness, family trouble, lack of popularity, unpleasant appearance, and so on. But there's no need to resign yourself to premature failure or to lower your standards just because you don't *think* you can compete with the head cheerleader or the football captain who went to Harvard, or because you had to borrow money from Uncle Sam to get through college, while Biff or Buffy has Uncle Rockefeller waiting with a job offer, or ready to make a few phone calls to assist in the job search.

It's all extraneous, because you're not out to seek approval, but fulfillment. Who really knows what someone else's potential is? Everyone who sets out to accomplish something, whether it's winning a swimming race or getting through medical school, hopes to succeed but isn't completely sure how his or her abilities match or exceed those of the competition.

But with each failed attempt, you learn about your abilities, what you're capable of and where your limitations lie. Because true failure is not falling down, but *staying* down. Even when you have achieved success (as you define it), don't assume you've fulfilled your potential and settle down. Keep striving to create new challenges.

Even when you've done your best, things may not always work out. Look at the "Live Aid" concert, for example, which was organized to raise money to relieve starvation after a terrible drought in Ethiopia. The concert was a tremendous success and raised millions of dollars, which went toward the purchase of 500,000 tons of grain. The grain subsequently rotted in warehouses on the shores of Ethiopia. The country lacked infrastructure, good roads, and transportation. The Ethiopians needed food and medical attention immediately, *not* crops for the following year. Unfortunately, it was a situation where a lot of bright, organized, and efficient people failed.

Part of failing is failing *smart*: knowing when to write off a product, an idea, a contact, or a job and learning from that experience. And move on to the next project. Remember, just when you're ready to conclude that "everything's been done before," the marketplace will eventually change enough to present you with a new opportunity or insight. In the meantime, keep your mind open, but don't let your brains fall out.

Because I am a former stock trader, many people ask me for stock tips. They have a thousand dollars that they would like to invest in the next superstock, pork bellies, or interest rate futures. If you have a thousand dollars to invest, invest it in yourself. When you've established a successful career, you will have plenty of money to buy a house, expensive clothes, stocks, a sports car, or whatever material objects you truly desire. Until then, make yourself the next superstock with the most growth and up-side potential. Take that thousand dollars and whether it's through purchasing books or magazine subscriptions, attending seminars, or traveling to speak with different authorities on subjects that interest you, invest in yourself for a guaranteed winner.

Remember, your opportunities can be found in your individuality. Inside you lies that unique advantage that will carry you to a winning position in your chosen field.

Resource Guide

Books

Adams, Bob, ed. The Job Bank Series: *Atlanta, Boston, Chicago, Dallas, Denver, Detroit, Florida, Houston, Los Angeles, Minneapolis, New York, Ohio, Philadelphia, San Francisco, St. Louis, Washington, D.C.* Boston: Bob Adams, Inc., 1992.

Boyer, Richard, and David Savageau. *Places Rated Almanac: Your Guide to Finding the Best Places to Live in America.* New York: Prentice-Hall, 1989.

Chambers, Dale. *Passport to Overseas Employment: 100,000 Job Opportunities Abroad.* Old Tappan, N.J.: Arco Books, 1990.

Eberts, Marjorie, and Margaret Gisler. *Careers for Culture Lovers and Other Artsy Types.* Lincolnwood, Ill.: NTC Publishing Group, 1992.

Field, Shelly. *Career Opportunities in the Sports Industry.* New York: Facts on File, Inc., 1991.

Frank, William S. *200 Letters for Job Hunters.* Berkeley: Ten Speed Press, 1990.

Fraz, Del, and Lázao Hernandez, *Work, Study, Travel Abroad: The Whole World Handbook.* 11th ed. New York: St. Martin's Press, 1992.

Gallagher, Richard P. *Your Small Business Made Simple.* New York: Doubleday, 1989.

Griffith, Susan. *Teaching English Abroad.* Princeton: Peterson's Guides, 1991.

―――. *Work Your Way Around the World.* 6th ed. Princeton: Peterson's Guides, 1993.

Kocher, Eric. *International Jobs: Where They Are and How to Get Them.* 2nd ed. Reading, Mass.: Addison-Wesley, 1989.

Krannich, Ron and Caryl. *The Almanac of American*

Government Jobs and Careers. Manassas, Va.: Impact Publications, 1991.

―――. *The Best Jobs for the 1990s and into the 21st Century.* Manassas, Va.: Impact Publications, 1992.

―――. *The Complete Guide to International Jobs and Careers.* Manassas, Va.: Impact Publications, 1990.

Maltzman, Jeffrey. *Jobs in Paradise: The Definitive Guide to Exotic Jobs Everywhere.* New York: Perennial Library, 1990.

Medley, H. Anthony. *Sweaty Palms: The Neglected Art of Being Interviewed.* Berkeley: Ten Speed Press, 1992.

Miller, Louise. *Careers for Nature Lovers and Other Outdoor Types.* Lincolnwood, Ill.: VGM Career Horizons, 1992.

Miller, Mary Fallon. *How to Get a Job with a Cruise Line.* St. Petersburg, Fla.: Ticket to Adventure, 1992.

Moskowitz, Milton, Robert Levering, and Michael Katz, eds. *Everybody's Business: A Field Guide to the 400 Leading Companies in America.* New York: Doubleday, 1990.

Parker, Yana. *The Resume Catalog: 200 Damn Good Examples.* Berkeley: Ten Speed Press, 1989.

Popcorn, Faith. *The Popcorn Report.* New York: Doubleday, 1991.

Rachlin, Harvey. *The TV and Movie Business.* New York: Harmony Books, 1991.

Sacharov, Al. *Offbeat Careers: The Directory of Unusual Work.* Berkeley: Ten Speed Press, 1988.

Sanborn, Robert. *How to Get a Job in Europe: The Insider's Guide.* Chicago: Surrey Books, 1991.

Stolze, William J. *Startup: An Entrepreneur's Guide to Launching and Managing a New Venture.* Rochester: Rock Beach Press, 1989.

Strauss, Erwin S. *How to Start Your Own Country.* Port Townsend, Wash.: Loompanics Unlimited, 1984.

Available at Large Libraries and Career Centers

Baker, Barbara, ed. *National Directory of Internships.* Raleigh, N.C.: National Society for Internships and Experiential Education, 1991.

Burek, Deborah M., ed. *Encyclopedia of Associations.* 27th ed. Detroit: Gale Research Inc., 1993.

The Career Source Encyclopedia. Danbury, Conn.: Grolier Educational Corp., 1992.

The Career Guide: Dun's Employment Opportunities Directory. Parsippany, N.J.: Dun's Marketing Services, 1993.

City and State Directories in Print. Detroit: Gale Research Inc., 1989.

Directory of U.S. Importers. New York: The Journal of Commerce, Inc., 1992.

Dun's Business Ranking. Parsippany, N.J.: Dun's Marketing Services, 1992.

Dun's Directory of Service Companies. Parsippany, N.J.: Dun's Marketing Services, 1993.

Dun's Industrial Guide: The Metalworking Directory. Parsippany, N.J.: Dun's Marketing Services. 1992.

Dun's Regional Business Directories. Parsippany, N.J.: Dun's Marketing Services, 1993.

Eldridge, Grant, ed. *Encyclopedia of Associations: Regional, State and Local Organizations.* Detroit: Gale Research Inc., 1992.

Hopke, William E., ed. *Encyclopedia of Careers and Vocational Guidance.* 8th ed. Garrett Park, Md.: Garrett Park Press, 1990.

Krol, John, ed. *Newsletters in Print.* 6th ed. Detroit: Gale Research Inc., 1993.

Magazines for Libraries. 7th ed. New Providence, N.J.: R. R. Bowker, 1992.

The Million Dollar Directory Series. Parsippany, N.J.: Dun's Marketing Services, 1993.

Moody's Industrial Manual. New York: Moody's Investors Service, Inc., 1991.

National Directory of Personnel Consultants. Alexandria, Va.: National Association of Personnel Consultants, 1993.

National Trade and Professional Association Directory. Washington, D.C.: Columbia Books, 1993.

Peterson's Guide to Colleges. Princeton: Peterson's Guides, 1993.

Standard and Poor's Register of Corporations, Directors and Executives. New York: Standard and Poor's, 1993.

Ulrich's International Periodicals Directory. 31st ed. New Providence, N.J.: R. R. Bowker, 1992–93.

Value Line Investment Survey. New York: Arnold Bernhard and Co. Published weekly.

Webster's New Biographical Dictionary. Springfield, Mass.: Merriam-Webster, 1988.

Who's Who in America. New Providence, N.J.: Reed Reference Publications, 1993.

Who's Who in America: Geographical/Professional Area Index. 47th ed. New Providence, N.J.: Reed Reference Publications, 1992.

Who's Who in Finance and Industry. 27th ed. New Providence, N.J.: Reed Reference Publications, 1991.

Information Available from the Government
[Available in many libraries. To inquire about cost before ordering, call (202)783-3238.]

Career Guide to Industries. Washington, D.C.: U.S. Department of Labor Statistics, 1993.

Dictionary of Occupational Titles. Washington, D.C.: U.S. Department of Labor Statistics, 1991.

The Occupational Outlook Handbook. Washington, D.C.: U.S. Department of Labor Statistics. Updated annually.

The Occupational Outlook Quarterly. Washington, D.C.: U.S. Department of Labor Statistics. Updated quarterly.

U.S. Industrial Outlook. Washington, D.C.: U.S. Department of Commerce, 1992.

Magazines and Trade Papers

Actors Resource. Greenwich, Conn.: ARN, Inc.

American Demographics. Ithaca, N.Y.: American Demographics.

Back Stage. New York, N.Y.: Billboard Publications, Inc.

Business Week. New York, N.Y.: McGraw-Hill.

De3B Reports for Small Business Management. New York, N.Y.: Dun & Bradstreet Corp.

The Economist. New York, N.Y. Economist Newspaper.

Entrepreneur. Anaheim, Calif.: Entrepreneur Group, Inc.

Entrepreneurial Woman. Irvine, Calif.: Entrepreneur Inc.

Forbes. New York, N.Y.: Forbes, Inc.

The Hollywood Reporter. Hollywood, Calif.: Billboard Publications, Inc.

International Business. Bellflower, Calif.: U.S. Business Trading Co.

Money. New York, N.Y.: Time, Inc.

New Business Opportunities. Irvine, Calif.: Entrepreneur Magazine.

Newsweek. New York, N.Y.: Newsweek, Inc.

Small Business Opportunities. New York, N.Y.: Harris Publications.

Successful Home Business. Woodland Hills, Calif.: The Mellinger Co.

Time. New York, N.Y.: Time, Inc.

Variety. New York, N.Y.: Cahner's Publishing.

World Trade. Irvine, Calif.: Taipan Press, Inc.

Catalogs, Digests, Guides, and Reports

Parness, J. M., ed. *The Complete Guide to Washington Internships*. Brooklyn: JMP Enterprises, 1988.

Lipinski, Alex. *Directory of Jobs and Careers Abroad*. 8th ed. Princeton: Peterson's Guides, 1993.

Directory of Overseas Summer Jobs. Princeton: Peterson's Guides, 1993.

Federal Jobs Digest. Ossining, N.Y.: Breakthrough Publications. Bi-monthly.

The Franchise Opportunities Guide. Washington, D.C.: The International Franchise Association. Updated annually.

The Information Catalog. New York: Find-S.V.P. Updated every two months.

Internships 1993. Princeton: Peterson's Guides, 1993.

Ross Reports Television: Casting, Scripts, Production. Long Island City, N.Y.: Television Index, Inc. Monthly.

The Small Business Development Catalog. Irvine, Calif.: The Entrepreneur Group, 1993.

Organizations

American Business Women's Association, 11 E. Hubbard St., Suite 200, Chicago, Ill. 60611, (312) 329-2512.

American Woman's Economic Development Corporation, 641 Lexington Avenue, New York, New York 10022, (212) 688-1900.

Chamber of Commerce of the United States of America, 1615 H St. NW, Washington, D.C. 20062, (202) 659-6000.

International Communication Association, P.O. Box 9589, Austin, Tex. 78766, (512) 454-8299.

International Television Association, 6311 N. O'Connor Rd., LB-51, Irving, Tex. 75039, (214) 869-1112.

National Association of Black and Minority Chambers of Commerce, 654 13th St., Oakland, Calif. 94612-1241, (415) 451-9231.

National Association of Sports Officials, 2017 Lathrop Ave., Racine, Wis. 53405, (414) 632-5448.

National Sportscasters and Sportswriters Association, P.O. Box 559, Salisbury, N.C. 28144, (703) 633-4275.

Index

accounting, 10, 126
adoption, 63
advertising, 10, 18, 27, 28, 59, 86,
    109, 146, 149, 151, 158
aerospace, 15
Africa, 40, 43
agriculture, 5, 22, 62, 87, 108
AIDS, 26, 58, 64–65
air conditioners, 53
airline industry, 8, 38, 67
Airport Channel, 15
alcohol, 17, 29, 42, 72
Allen, Woody, 11–12, 156
Altman, B., 9
ambition, 47, 152, 160
American Airlines, 8
American Demographics (magazine),
    53–54
"America's Most Wanted" (TV
    show), 57
Amnesty International, 27
Anaheim Marketing, 92
Animal Grahams, 23
annual company reports, 104, 107,
    151
answering machines, 73
antiquarian bookselling, 53
Apple Computer, 42
appliance repair, 109
aptitude, 93–94
architecture, 10, 124
Argentina, 40
art restoration, 53
arts, 53, 131
Asian markets, 40, 42–43
astronomy, 11
AT&T, 7, 55, 124
Austin, Texas, 101

Bach, Richard, *Jonathan Livingston
    Seagull*, 159

Back Stage (magazine), 93
bakeries, 73, 91–92
banking, 5, 10, 12, 13, 14, 19, 22,
    28–29, 34, 41, 110–11, 126,
    147
bankruptcy, 9
Barbie doll, 70
Bean, L. L., 68
Bell South, 8
bicycle tour planning, 62
BIDS (Business Improvement
    Districts), 33
biogenetic products, 22
biotechnology, 22
birth control, 62, 64–65
Body Shop, The, 27–28
Boise, Idaho, 100
bonuses, 139
bookkeeping, 132
Brazil, 40
breads and cakes, 73, 91–92
Brooks Brothers, 41
Burger King, 56
Bush, George, 58
business(es)
    entrepreneurship in, 44–61
    environmental awareness in, 19–
        26
    global, 34–36, 37–43
    high technology, 5–16, 108
    privatization, 29–36
    problems as opportunities, 62–73
    and social consciousness, 26–29
    trend analysis, 54–61
    see also specific businesses
business administration, 48
business associations, 104–105
business cards, 137
business communications, 13
Business Week (magazine), 11, 42,
    58, 100

cable television, 6, 13–15, 44, 48, 68–69
California, 7, 28, 31, 65, 99, 100
Canada, 24, 40, 42
capitalism, 34–35, 37
car(s), 17–18, 51, 67–68, 71, 133
  electric, 7, 25
  phones, 6, 8, 110
  rentals, 10
  repair, 51, 81, 109
  safety, 17–18, 58
career development, 77–163
  and education plans, 120–28
  finding a job, 141–55
  information gathering for, 113–19
  natural talent in, 89–97
  occupational pitfalls, 82–87
  specific fields, 98–112
  and street smarts, 156–62
  and true calling, 78–81
  volunteer work, 129–40
career entrepreneurship, 44–61, 116–17, 141, 145, 156
Career Guide to Industries, 102–103
Careers for Culture Lovers and Other Artsy Types (Eberts and Gisler), 52
Carter, Jimmy, 30
Carter-Wallace, 64
catalytic converters, 21
catering, 52, 61, 91
chamber of commerce, 104, 106, 116
change, 86, 87–88
Chavez, Ed, 92
Checkout Channel, 15
Chicago, 28
Chicken of the Sea, 27
child care, 63, 66–67, 108
Chile, 40
chimney sweeping, 61
China, 34–35, 40, 42, 110
choreography, 52
Christian Science Monitor, 20
Christmas tree sales, 61
Citibank, 42
cities, jobs in, 100–102
Clean Air Act (1990), 20
Clean-Flo Laboratories, 23
cleaning services, 52
Clinton, Lu, 91
clowns, 90

CNN, 6, 15, 42, 48
Coca-Cola, 41
Cohen, Adam, 54
Cold War, 39
  end of, 37
Colgate-Palmolive Company, 41
college, 10, 11, 82, 103, 120–28
  planning for, 120–28
comedy, 69
common sense, 47–51
Commonwealth of Independent States (CIS), 38–40; *see also* Russia
communism, 34, 35, 37
Competitive Advantage of Nations, The (Porter), 10
Complete Guide to International Jobs and Careers, The (Krannick), 148
Comprehensive Employment and Training Act, 30
computer(s), 6, 7–13, 53, 90, 100–102, 108, 133, 135, 138
  for children, 53, 56
  graphics, 13
  growth of, 7-13
  programming, 7, 11, 13, 90
  sales and marketing, 7
  shopping, 8–9, 13
Computerland, 41
condoms, 61, 64
construction, 10, 51
consumer finance, 10
consumerism, 3–5, 16–19
  global, 37–43
consumer trends, 53–61
convenience, 69–70
Coors Brewing, 41
cosmetics, 51, 113–14
cover letters, 128, 141, 148 150, 151
credit cards, 10
credit reporting, 10
crime, 57–58
crises, easing, 64–67
Cross Creek Recreational Products, Incorporated, 65
customized clothing, 53
custom software, 10

D. C. Otherwise, 131
dance, 52

D & B Reports for Small Business Management (magazine), 52
day spas, 53
decorum, maintaining, 157
dentists, 56
Department of Agriculture, 22
Department of Labor, 6, 78, 99, 102
DHL, 32
Dictionary of Occupational Titles, 78
Digital Equipment, 41
Dinkins, David, 64
direct marketing, 8–9
Directory of Overseas Summer Jobs, 148
Directory of United States Importers, 51–52
discount stores, 18–19
Discovery Zone, 18
Disneyland, 42
doctors, 82, 124
Domino's Pizza, 42
driveway sealing, 61
drug testing, 26
Dun's Business Rankings, 102
Dun's Directory of Service Companies, 146
Dun's Industrial Guide: The Metalworking Directory, 51
Du Pont, 42

easing crises, 64–67
Eastern Europe, 19, 22–23, 34, 38–39, 41–42
Eastman Kodak, 41
Economist, The (magazine), 6, 9, 34, 58, 111
economy, 3, 79, 111
  changing structures, 5–13, 46, 50–51
  future growth of, 108
  global, 34–36, 37–44
Edison Project, 33–34
education, 5, 10, 11, 15, 33–34, 47, 63, 82–83, 102, 103, 109, 116, 120–28, 134, 144
  graduate, 125, 126–28
  planning for, 120–28
electronics, 72
employers, locating, 144–48
Encyclopedia of Associations, 104, 105
En Fleur, 90–91

engineering, 10, 11, 12, 21, 32–33, 124
entertainment industry, 10, 13–16, 43, 59, 68–69, 93, 96, 110, 118, 153
Entrepreneur (magazine), 52
Entrepreneurial Woman (magazine), 53
entrepreneurship, career, 44–61, 116–17, 141, 145, 156
entry-level positions, 142–44, 153–54
environmental awareness, 17, 18, 19–29, 35, 56, 59
environmental industry, 10, 12, 19–27, 58, 61, 108
errand-running, 133, 135, 152
ESPN, 42
Esprit de Corp, 28
ethanol, 21
ethics, business, 26–29
Euro-Disneyland, 42
Europe, 34, 42, 43, 111, 147
exercise, 15, 55
experience, importance of, 129–40
export markets, 6, 11, 22, 35, 36, 39–44
express delivery services, 32, 72

fads, 59–60, 118
failure, 78, 160–62
family, 4–5, 66–67, 82–83, 103, 148
Far Eastern Economic Review, 147–48
fashion, 3–4, 19, 49, 53, 54, 68, 73, 91, 107
fast food, 10, 38, 51, 56, 68
faxes, 6, 9
Federal Express, 14, 32, 71
Federal Interstate Highway System, 32–33
Federal Jobs Digest, 147
fields, career, 98–112
finance, 28–29, 110–11, 153–54
Financial Times, 146
finding a job, 141–55
fire prevention, 65–66, 115
First Environmental Bank and Trust, Portsmouth, N.H., 22
Fitness Channel, 15
flea markets, 51
Florida, 33, 100
flower vending, 61

Food and Drug Administration, 25
food preparation, 53, 61, 73, 81,
    91–92
Forbes magazine, 32, 48, 146
Ford, Henry, 10, 73, 159
Ford Motor Co., 72
foreign languages, 147
Fortune magazine, 146
Fox Television, 65
France, 43
Franchise Opportunities Guide, The,
    61
friends, 82, 103, 113, 142

Gallagher, Richard, *Your Small
    Business Made Simple,* 61
Galson Remediation Corp., 22
gambling, 81
games, 81
Ganz, Nancy, 50
garbage collection, 33
gardening, 81, 84
garment-bag manufacturing, 91
Gates, William, 90
Gemstar, 92
General Electric, 8, 23
general maintenance jobs, 108
General Mills, 132
generic products, 19
Germany, 34, 147
gift basket service, 61
global consumerism, rise of, 37–44
global pollution, 22–23
global privatization, 34–36, 37–44
goals, career, 98–99, 139
government agencies, 7, 30–33, 65
Government Job Finder, The, 128
graduate school, 10, 11, 125, 126–
    28
Grave Line Tours, 91
Great Depression, 30
greenhouse effect, 20
green products, 23–25
Gretzky, Wayne, 140
growth industries, 108–12
guidance counselors, 83, 134
Gulf War, 6, 39

Haagen-Dazs, 42, 51
haircutting, 52–53
handicapped, problems of the, 72
Handler, Ruth, 71

Harmon, Larry, 90
health care, 5, 10, 12, 17, 32, 53,
    54, 59, 65–68, 69, 108, 126,
    131
health crises, 65–68
Healthdyne Incorporated, 66
Hefty trash bags, 24
herb farming, 62
Hewlett-Packard, 13
high school, 10, 48, 83, 103, 122,
    125
high technology, 5–16, 45, 108
Hipslip, 50
hobbies, 79–80, 86–87, 88
Holiday Inn, 42
Hollywood Reporter, The (magazine),
    93
homelessness, 65
home remodeling, 61
Hooker, Richard, *M°A°S°H°,* 160
hospital(s), 31, 32, 85–86, 114, 144
    management, 10
hotels, 10, 11, 42, 53, 110
hours, working, 18
housing, 63–64, 65, 95
How to Start Your Own Country
    (Strauss), 128
Hyatt Hotels, 42

IBM, 8
immigration, 4
India, 40, 43
individuality, 155, 163
Indonesia, 40
industrial revolution, 5, 118
industries, choice of, 98–112
infertility, 59
Infonet, 8
information/data, 10
Information Catalog, The, 60
information processing, 10
infrastructure, 32–33
initiating projects, 137–39
In-Process Technologies, 22
insurance, 5, 10, 32, 152
Integrated Health Services, 32
International Business, 147
international career opportunities,
    147–48
*International Jobs: Where They Are
    and How to Get Them* (Kocher),
    147

International Waste Management Systems, 23
internships, 127, 130–40, 142, 150
interviews, job, 141–42, 144, 150–53
investment banking, 10, 110–11, 126

Japan, 15–16, 24, 34, 39, 42, 111, 147
Jell-O, 73
Job Bank Series, 127–28
job-hunting procedures, 141–55
Jonathan Livingston Seagull (Bach), 159
journalism, 86, 115, 131, 147

Kempf, Martine, 65
Keynes, John Maynard, 3
Knight, Philip, 48–49
Korea, 40, 41
Kraft, 41
Kroc, Ray, 160
Kwoh, Daniel, 92

labor unions, 104
Land's End, 9
lawyers, 13, 82, 108, 124, 126, 131, 147
leadership, 88, 139
leasing, 10
left-handed people, 70
Leonard, Sugar Ray, 89
Levi's, 41, 47–48
libraries, 31, 78, 79, 144–46
licenses, 144
Life magazine, 131
lifestyle, 158
Lillian Vernon, 9
"Live Aid" concert, 161–62
Loblaw's, 24
locating employers, 144–48
locations, job, 99–102, 146
London International Group, 64
long-distance phone services, 55–56
Los Angeles, 28
Los Angeles Times, 22
luck, 88

M.B.A. degree, 11, 47, 126–27
McDonald's, 15, 34, 160
machinery, 51

Macy's, 9
Madonna, 42, 49, 118
magazines, 52–53, 58–59, 79, 93, 106–107, 116, 146, 157; *see also specific magazines*
Magazines for Libraries (Katz), 58
Mail Boxes Etc., 71
mailing lists, 54
mail-order catalogs, 9
Make-Up Art Cosmetics, 26–27
Mall of America, Bloomington, Minnesota, 63
mall schools, 63
management consulting, 10, 21, 147
manufacturing jobs, 5, 6, 12, 20, 51
marine biology, 126
marketing, 109, 127, 145, 149
Martech USA, 23
M°A°S°H° (Hooker), 159
mass media, 6, 27, 56–59,
rise of, 13–16
mass transportation, 31
MasterCard, 26
mathematics, 11
Mattel, Incorporated, 70
MCI, 26, 55
Medicaid, 32
Members Only, 28
Merrill Lynch, 132
Mexico, 40, 110
Microsoft, 90
military, 39, 40, 68, 77, 115
Million Dollar Directory, The, 146
Minneapolis, 64, 101
Money magazine, 80, 123
money management, 10
monitoring equipment, 21
Moody's Industrial Manual, 102, 145
Morita, Akio, 73
Motorola, 42
movies, 13–16, 43, 56, 68, 93, 110
moving, 80–81
MTV, 14, 42
Multimedia, 15
music, 15, 16, 43, 52, 56, 110, 118
mutual funds, 28–29, 111

National Directory of Personnel Consultants, 146
National Enquirer, The, 59
natural resources, 11

natural talent, 89–97
Nature Company, 24
need, creating a, 73–74
networking, 103–106, 113, 137, 142, 148, 157
Newborn Channel, 15
New Business Opportunities (magazine), 52
New Hampshire, 22
New Jersey, 19, 100, 101
Newsletters in Print, 58
newspapers, 8, 13, 14, 57–59, 79, 106–107, 116, 146; *see also specific newspapers*
Newsweek magazine, 23, 58
New York, 19–20, 49–50, 64, 65, 99, 106
New York Times, The, 38, 41, 57
New York Times Magazine, The, 23
Nick at Nite, 68
Nike, 48–49
Nixon, Richard, 30
nonalcoholic beverages, 70–71
nutrition, 17, 114
NYNEX, 8

observations, business, 45, 47–61
obsolescence, 71–72
Occupational Outlook Quarterly (U.S. Department of Labor) 7, 78, 79, 108, 123
occupational pitfalls, 82–87
Offbeat Careers: The Directory of Unusual Work (Sacharov), 112
operations analysis, 12
opportunities, problems as, 62–73, 160–62
organizational consulting, 53
organizations, trade, 104–105, 116
Orlando, Florida, 100

Pacific Telesis, 8
packaging restrictions, 112
parental expectations, 82–83
Parker, Nell Caitlin, 90–91
Parker, Yana, 141
Parnassus, 28, 29
part-time employment, 153
People magazine, 58, 95
Pepsi-Cola, 38–39, 41
personal style, 88

personnel departments, 104, 149–50
pet care, 54, 61
Peterson's Guide to Internships, 131
Petit, Parker H., 65
Philadelphia, 101
phobia treatment, 66
phone services, 26, 55–56, 61, 65, 110, 124, 132
physics, 11
Pilzer, Paul Zane, *Unlimited Wealth*, 3
pitfalls, occupational, 82–87
Pizza Hut, 38, 42
Places Rated Almanac: Your Guide to Finding the Best Places to Live in America (Boyer and Savageau), 80
Polaroid Corporation, 21, 38
politics, 5, 14, 28, 34–36, 56, 86, 94, 97, 118, 131, 147
global, 34–36
pollution control, 10, 12, 19–26, 58, 62, 108
pool maintenance, 61, 116–17
Popcorn, Faith, *The Popcorn Report*, 53
Porter, Michael, *The Competitive Advantage of Nations*, 10
Postal Service, 30–31, 32
Post-it Notes, 70
Premiere magazine, 15
presentation, importance of, 151–53
Princeton, New Jersey, 101
privatization, 29–36
global, 34–36, 37–44
problems, as opportunities, 62–73, 160–62
productivity, worker, 6, 11
promotions, 109, 139, 143–44
Provo, Utah, 101
public companies, 107
public relations, 10, 151–52
public works, 30
publishing, 139–40, 147, 159, 160

QVC, 13–14

radio, 59
railways, 34, 108

Ram Broadcasting, 8
real estate, 28, 35, 38, 39, 110, 111
Real Goods Company, 24
real people, 117–19
Reebok, 49
religion, 35
repair and maintenance, 5, 10, 51,
    61, 81, 108, 109
research, 21, 144–45
restaurants, 49–50, 51, 52, 56, 84–
    85, 110
*Resumé Catalog: 200 Damn Good
    Examples, The* (Parker), 141
resumés, 103, 128, 130, 131, 139,
    140, 141–42, 143, 147, 148–51
retirement, 46
Risky Business (movie), 68
Rivers, Joan, 95
Roddick, Anita, 27–28
role models, 117–18
Rolodexes, 138
*Ross Reports Television: Casting,
    Scripts, Production*, 93
Russia, 34, 37–40
    economy of, 37–39, 57
Ruth, Babe, 160

SAAB, 18
salaries, 83, 95, 103, 114, 120, 135,
    140
Salomon Brothers, 27
Salt Lake City, Utah, 102
San Diego, 100
San Francisco, 28, 99
Schmidt, Benno, 33
science, 11, 94, 108, 124
security systems, 57–58, 109
self-employment, 52–61, 116
seminar promoting, 61
service industries, 5–6, 10–13, 52
Sharper Image, The, 73
Sheraton Hotels, 42
shopping, 18–19, 52, 63, 84, 109,
    110
    personal, 61
    television, 8–9, 13–15
sign-making services, 71–72
Silly Putty, 73
"60 Minutes" (TV show), 56–57
skateboarding, 60
*Small Business Development Catalog,
    The*, 53

Small Business Opportunities
    (magazine), 52
"small indulgence" products, 53
Smith, Greg, 91
Snack Food (magazine), 106
social consciousness, 26–29
social problems, 62–64
Sony Corporation, 73
South America, 40, 43
South Shore Bank, Chicago, 28
sports, 16, 60, 79, 89, 140, 160
Sprint, 55
*Standard and Poor's Register of
    Corporations, Directors and
    Executives*, 145
Star-Kist, 24, 27
startup companies, 154–55
steel, 5, 6, 29
Stephenson, W. David, 20–21
stock market(s), 35, 36, 105–106,
    153–54, 162
    global, 37–38, 40
street smarts, 156–62
strengths, career, 85
stress reduction, 109
student loans, 127
success, 159–60
Successful Home Business
    (magazine), 52
Sudden Infant Death Syndrome,
    65
*Sweaty Palms: The Neglected Art of
    Being Interviewed* (Medley),
    141–42

talent, natural, 89–97
taxes, 35, 60, 111, 118, 128, 152
teachers, 47, 52, 61, 94, 109, 125,
    126, 131, 134, 142, 147
telecommunications, 110
television, 6, 8–9, 13–16, 18, 42,
    56–57, 59, 68, 93, 96, 110
    shopping by, 8–9, 13–15
    trends, 57, 59, 68–73
temporary help, 10, 153
tests, 83
Texas, 22, 101
Thailand, 40, 42, 110
thank-you notes, 150, 151
theater, 52
3M Corporation, 21
Time magazine, 58, 131

Time Warner, 131
tobacco, 17, 29
toll-collection systems, 7
Tomlin, Lily, 124–25
Top Gun (movie), 68
tourism, 99, 110
toys, 54, 66, 71, 81
Toys R Us, 41–42
trade organizations, 104–105, 116
training, 10, 11, 114, 129, 130–40
transportation, 5, 7–8, 10, 25, 31–33, 34, 54, 79, 87, 110, 138
trend analysis, 53–61
Tropicana Products, Incorporated, 26
trucking, 110
true calling, 78–81
Tucson, Arizona, 100
Turner, Ted, 48
Turner Broadcasting System, 15, 43, 48
tutoring, 61
TV and Movie Business, The (Rachlin), 93
typesetting, 7
types of careers, 98–112

Ulrich's International Periodicals Directory, 58
unemployment, 30, 142
United Nations, 147
Unlimited Wealth (Pilzer), 3
unusual careers, 111–12, 115–16
UPS, 32, 71
USSR, 30, 34
  demise of, 5
US West, 8
Utah, 101, 102
utility bill auditing, 53

vacations, 54, 102, 117, 136
"value-added" concept, 12
Value Line Investment Survey, 145
Vandermolen, Mimi, 71
Vapor Canada, Incorporated, 7–8

Variety (magazine), 93
VCR Plus, 92
Vencor, Incorporated, 32
venture capitalists, 22
veterinarians, 54, 124
Victoria's Secret, 8
videos, 15, 16, 43, 59, 61, 73, 92, 110, 127, 157
Visa, 26
vision, 47–48
volunteer work, 88, 115, 124, 129–40
Volvo, 18

Wackenhut Corporation, 33
wage levels, 10
waitressing, 142
Wall Street Journal, The, 22, 50, 58
Wal-Mart, 24
war, 68
Washington, D.C., 100, 131
Washington Post, 21
waste disposal and management, 10, 12, 19–26, 58, 61, 108
weaknesses, career, 85
Webster's New Biographical Dictionary, 117–18
weddings, 70–71
When Harry Met Sally (movie), 56
Whittle, Christopher, 33
Who's Who in America, 117–18
Who's Who in America: Geographical/ Professional Area Index, 96
Who's Who in Finance and Industry, 145
World Link, 147–48
World Trade, 147–48

Yellow Pages, 105, 112, 146
Yeltsin, Boris, 34
Your Small Business Made Simple (Gallagher), 60
Yuen, Henry, 92

Zabar's, 8